Early 20th Century.

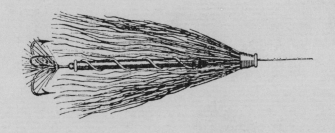

Contemporary

FLY-TYING PROBLEMS
AND THEIR ANSWERS

SPECKLED HEN WING QUILL

BROWN HEN WING QUILL

HEN PHEASANT QUILL

WHITE DUCK QUILL

GREY DUCK QUILL

MALLARD WHITE TIP BLUE QUIL

HEN PHEASANT TAIL

SPECKLED PARTRIDGE TAIL

SPECKLED GROUSE TAIL

GREY DRAKE

FRENCH
PARTRIDGE
HACKLE

BROWN
PARTRIDGE
HACKLE

WOODCOCK
HACKLE

GROUSE
HACKLE

SNIPE
HACKLE

FEATHERS FOR TROUT FLIES

Fly-tying Problems

and their answers

text by John Veniard
drawings by Donald Downs

Crown Publishers, Inc., New York

FIRST PUBLISHED 1970
BY A. AND C. BLACK LIMITED
4, 5 AND 6 SOHO SQUARE LONDON WIV 6AD

TEXT © 1970 JOHN VENIARD
DRAWINGS © 1970 DONALD DOWNS

FIRST PUBLISHED IN THE UNITED STATES
OF AMERICA 1972 BY CROWN PUBLISHERS, INC.

LIBRARY OF CONGRESS CATALOG CARD NUMBER: 79-187579

ISBN: 0-517-507870

SECOND PRINTING, OCTOBER, 1973

DEDICATION

To all fly fishermen and fly-tyers, particularly those whose interest and ideas have made such a major contribution to this book, and to David Downs, who evinced both interest and encouragement in the production of the drawings.

Printed in the United States of America

Contents

FOREWORD TO THE 1970 EDITION

It has always been a personal theory of mine that the best way to teach fly tying, other than by direct instruction, was by enlarged and exaggerated black-and-white illustration. Unfortunately, my own ability to illustrate fell far short of what I thought was necessary, and although I have written many thousands of words describing the craft of fly tying, I was never able to back them up with drawings which would have simplified to the reader what I was trying to put across.

You can imagine, therefore, how pleased I was when I met Donald Downs, my collaborator on this volume, who was not only a fisherman and a fly tyer, but also an illustrator of the first order. Add to this the fact that he was able to apply his training as an architect to the illustrated construction of all the aspects of fly tying, and one can then realise how great his contribution and collaboration has been.

We first worked together on my book *Reservoir and Lake Flies*, and it was from that joint effort that I culled the idea to reproduce my *Fly-Tying Problems* in the way I had always hoped it would be.

I have tried to retain the descriptive material as closely as possible to the original articles which resulted in the first book, and this was made easier by the fact that Don's drawings are so descriptive in themselves that they need very little written instruction to back them up.

Whether I am right in this assumption can be left only to the opinions of readers, but I am very confident that there will be few who do not agree with me.

1970   JOHN VENIARD

PREFACE

This book was the result of a series of articles which appeared in the *Fishing Gazette* between October 1956 and February 1957. It was not meant to be just another book on fly tying, although it is concerned entirely with this subject, but a collection of suggested methods of overcoming those parts of fly tying which give rise to difficulty to all of us at some time or another.

Many of the suggestions and ideas contained herein were given to me by a number of fly-tying enthusiasts, and I have named them in the chapters concerned. Much credit must be given to their ideas and ingenuity, and I am sure that they will be very pleased to know that this book, in conjunction with any good fly-tying manual, should enable anyone to tie flies without recourse to individual tuition.

My personal advice to anyone who ties flies, regardless of the stage of proficiency he or she may have reached, is: if ever you come up against any difficulty, concentrate on the difficulty until it is overcome. In other words, the particularly difficult problem should be practised until it no longer presents any difficulty. It is not necessary to follow slavishly any instructions, written or otherwise, that purport to show how it is done. A little careful thought, several attempts by trial and error, and above all a little patience, will soon simplify every problem you are likely to come up against.

I would also like to express my appreciation of the late Mr. Marston, who was editor of the *Fishing Gazette* at the time the articles were published, for his co-operation in the publication of the articles concerned.

In conclusion I would like to quote some words from one of the many letters I received from Capt. the Hon. R. Coke during the publication of the articles, and who made a considerable contribution to the ideas and suggestions:

"I welcome any endeavour to persuade fishermen to tie their own flies, not only for reasons of economy, as it is a great hobby and one that could do something to halt universal spinning, especially for trout, which I consider an outrage."

JOHN VENIARD

INTRODUCTION

There must be many fishermen who are in the habit of reading angling periodicals who have not failed to notice the increased interest in, and practice of, fly fishing in this country. This post-war upsurge is due to several reasons, not the least being that the old idea that fly fishing is a rich man's hobby is fast dying a long overdue death. Increased travel facilities, and hotels which cater for fishermen only, in areas where fly fishing is, in the main, all that is allowed, have all helped to spread the cult. Moreover, having once tried this delightful method of angling, most fishermen are keen to continue. Nor is fly fishing confined to game fish as it used to be, now that so many coarse-fish anglers have discovered how they can increase the range of their angling methods.

This increase in the numbers of fly fishermen has brought one factor to light which never bothered earlier devotees, namely, the shortage of well-made flies. I am not saying that good flies are not made any more, as this is definitely not true, but the fact is that although the demand for flies has considerably increased, the number of tyers making them is less than before the last war. Many were lost to other industries during the war, and there have been few replacements. It is therefore impossible for present-day tyers to cope with the demand the new interest has created and also fulfil their export commitments. The demand for British-made flies is still world wide, even though many countries which never had tyers of their own are now building up this trade.

To my mind, the fly is a more important part of the "team" than the rod, reel, line or cast, for without it these expensive items might just as well be left at home for all the effect they can have on one's catch. I know that the fly cannot be presented to the fish

11

without them also, that is why I used the word "team", but the big difference is that they cost many pounds collectively, whereas the fly is comparatively cheap. Even with today's inflated prices and Purchase Tax, it is still possible for the amateur, after he has bought his fly-tying equipment of course, to sit down and make a fly for a very reasonable sum. It would be difficult to state an exact figure, as this must vary with the type of fly being tied, the range being between a simple hackled fly like the "Blue Upright" for instance, and a complex salmon fly such as the "Jock Scott".

It is this fact which is the point of this preamble. There is only one answer if one cannot buy the fly one wants—"do it yourself". There is not a fly in the book the amateur cannot tie once the necessary know-how has been acquired, and there are many books on the market devoted solely to imparting this knowledge.

In spite of this vast storehouse of knowledge, however, there always seems to be one or other part of the craft which eludes the would-be fly tyer, and this results in many giving up before they really even got started. With myself it was the putting on of wings, a stage in fly tying which causes most of us trouble in the early stages. Others have difficulty with other aspects, of course, as I know from the correspondence I receive from old hands and new ones, who want to know some little thing or other.

It is these few minor difficulties which have probably built up the old prejudice that fly tying is too difficult for the non-professional, but it is amazing how easy the whole business becomes once one has passed one's personal hurdle.

I know for a fact that some beginners are put off by the appearance of their early efforts, which is quite ridiculous, for no matter how expert one may become, the first flies one ties usually look terrible. A single lesson from an expert can be of more value than all the books, but I do maintain that it is possible to teach fly tying by the written word and clear illustration, provided it is done properly.

There is also the question of knowing the right materials to use, as some dressings given in books can be very vague on this subject. For instance, if the wing of the fly calls for a mallard feather, this could be any one of five different feathers from the mallard which are used for winging purposes.

I have always felt that if fly tyers had some means of having their questions answered, it would be of great help not only to the questioner, but to many who have been put off merely because there was some small stage in the procedure they could not master, or did not know what materials to use. I do not mean that they should have another series of fly tying books inflicted upon them, but I do think that there must be many, beginners and old hands, who would be pleased to take advantage of one devoted solely to the detailed description of the more tricky points of fly tying, descriptions of materials to be used, and suggestions as to what materials can be used as substitutes for those that are scarce or unobtainable.

The answers to these questions may result in many doubtful starters becoming proficient enthusiasts, which would be doing them a favour, as there is no doubt that fly tying is one of the most interesting and pleasurable hobbies allied to the gentle art.

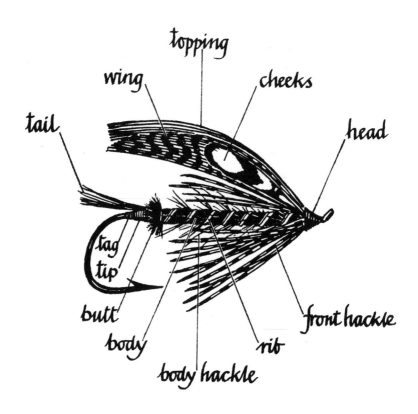

topping

wing

cheeks

tail

head

tag
tip

butt

body

body hackle

rib

front hackle

THE PARTS OF A FLY

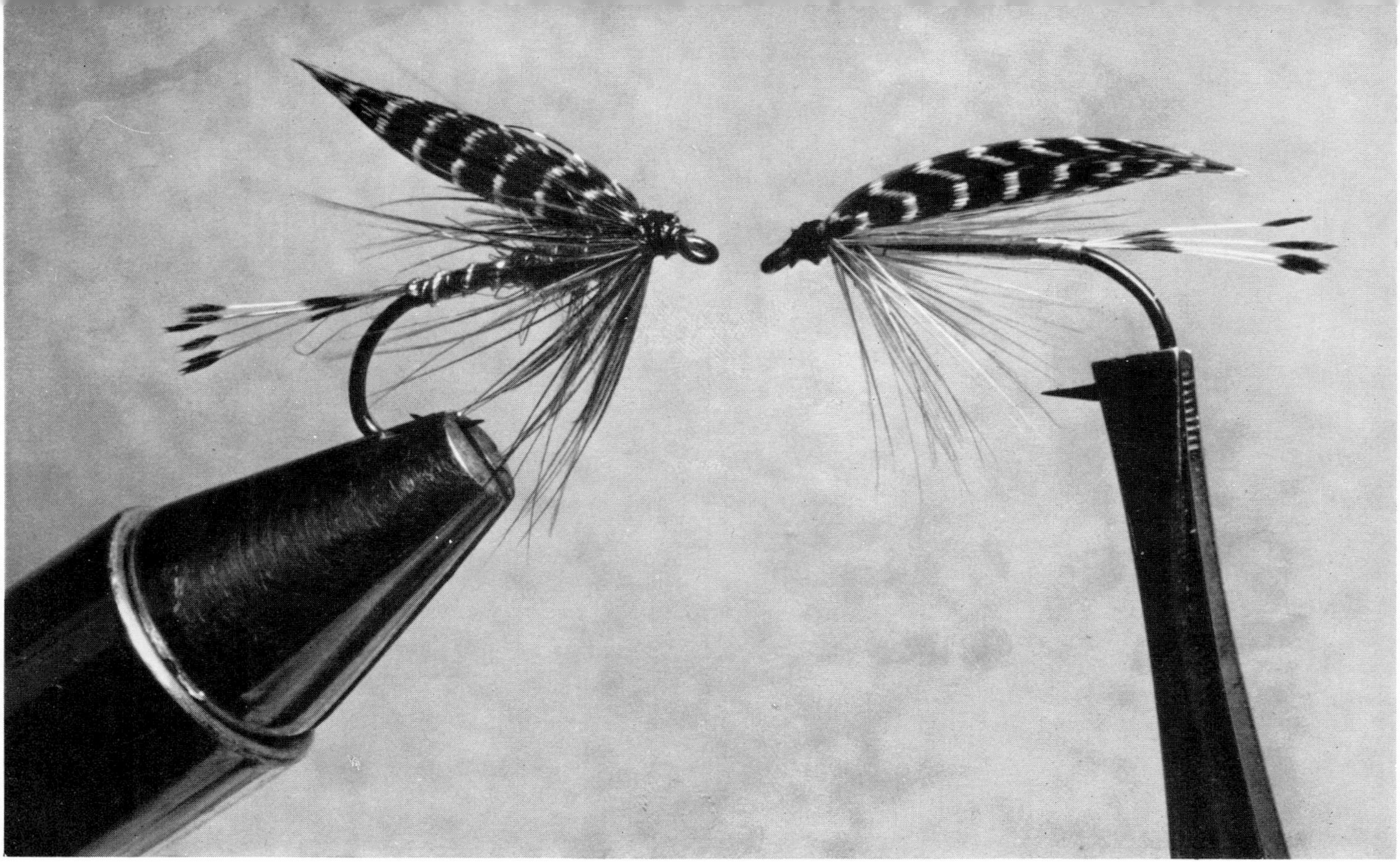

STYLES OF WINGING

TANDEM HOOK LURE

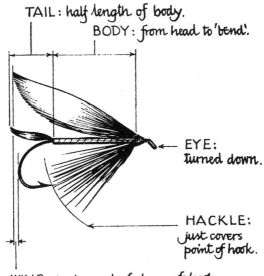

TAIL: half length of body.

BODY: from head to 'bend'.

EYE: turned down.

HACKLE: just covers point of hook.

WING: just proud of shape of hook.

WET FLY

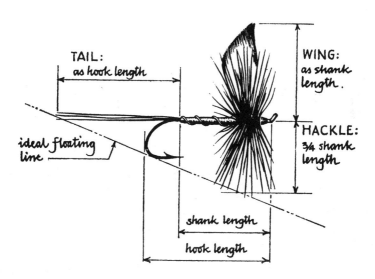

TAIL: as hook length

WING: as shank length.

HACKLE: 3/4 shank length

ideal floating line

shank length

hook length

DRY FLY

THE PROPORTIONS OF THE FLY

CHAPTER 1. WINGS AND WINGING

The tying on of wings is usually the first difficulty encountered by the amateur fly tyer.

Like many other apparently involved processes, once one knows how, it is simplicity itself. The main difficulty appears to be how to impart this knowledge by the written word and illustration, so that the beginner is left in no doubt as to how it is done. There are several books of instruction which do this quite well, so all I can do is endeavour to make the explanation simpler still.

Tools for winging are obtainable, and although I prefer to use my fingers, mainly for reasons of speed, these tools can put a well-shaped wing on to the hook and are ideal in demonstrating the technique required to do so.

The secret, if secret it be, of a well-tied wing, is to bring each fibre of the slips of feathers used down on top of the fibre beneath it, without any divergence from the vertical. This is achieved by forming a loop of the tying silk over the wing, gripping the hook, silk and wing firmly, and then drawing the tying silk tight. Three tight turns should be made in this manner before removing the fingers. Do not pull the silk tighter after removing the fingers, as this tends to pull the wing over to the far side of the hook.

The position of the fingers for this operation is shown opposite.

The procedure when using winging pliers is as follows: prepare the left and right wings and place them in the tool, the spring tension of which will keep them in position. Place the tool near the hook and then pass at least two turns of the tying silk through the eye of the tool. Place the tool on top of the hook-shank where the wing is to be tied in and then draw this silk tight. Now comes what to my mind is the most important part of the instruction. Hold the tool by the jaws which grip the wing, and not by its top. Not

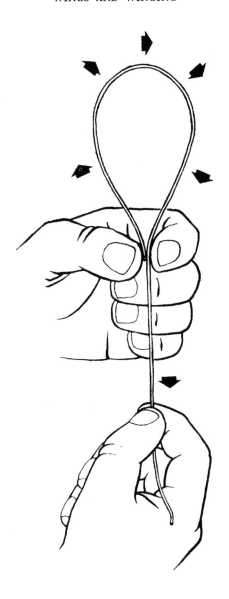

too tightly or you will find it impossible to draw the wing down. This will ensure that each fibre comes down one on top of the other, and also demonstrates what you would do if you were not using the winging tool. Also, most important, put another turn of silk round the hook-shank to ensure that the wing will not move when the tool is removed.

If it is a wet-fly or a salmon fly being tied, the surplus end of the wing can now be cut off and several turns of silk taken over the remaining butt to form the head.

If a dry-fly is being tied, the wing slips will have been placed so that the points turn outwards. When the tool is removed the wings must be again gripped firmly (not including the hook this time), raised to the vertical, a couple of turns put round their base, and then another round the hook-shank. This will keep them in the upright position, and another figure-of-eight turn between them will keep them separated. At all times keep the tying silk taut, and make all turns of silk as tightly as the strength of tying silk will allow. Slackness at any time is fatal.

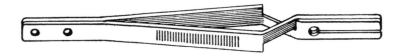

When I make my own dry-flies I prefer to tie the wings in the forward position. That is, with the wings pointing over the eye of the hook and not to the rear when they are tied in. The procedure for tying them in is exactly the same, except that the wings are tied in before the body and tail, etc., instead of last, as in the usual method. This means that the wing can be tied in nearer the eye, and the butt can be covered by the body material. It is only necessary to wind the hackle at the back of the wing instead of the back and the front, which makes a much neater job in my opinion. It is, however, even more essential that the wings be fixed firmly in the upright position, as there are no hackle fibres in front of the wings to assist in keeping them upright.

Before starting to tie his winged flies the beginner will do well to practise the winging procedure on its own. To do this I advocate a largish hook, and a wing material consisting of fibres which stay well together. The best one I know is the primary feather from the wild duck (mallard) wing, and with the help of the foregoing the absolute tyro should be able to form a reasonable wing after several attempts.

With regard to the softer materials used for winging some sea-trout and salmon flies, such as teal flank and mallard shoulder feathers, the procedure with these is exactly the same except that the firm approach is even more essential. It also helps if double thicknesses of these feathers are used, i.e. two slips from a left-hand feather for one side of the wing, and two slips from a right-hand feather for the other, as this prevents that "wispy" effect one often gets when using these feathers.

The natural shape of the feathers one uses for wings can also be utilised to give the desired shape to the wings. If the top edge of the wing slips is left at the top when the wing is tied in, the resulting wing will be as below left. If put on upside down the result is as below right.

I think this would be the best stage to introduce Don's instructional drawings, which are as follows:

No. 1. Two roughly equal feathers, "paired".

Fig. 2. An exaggerated elevation drawing showing the interlocking fibres on the wing "herls" which we must utilise to keep our tied-in wings neat and tidy. The cross-section drawing illustrates the natural curve of the feather fibres on the quill, which we also utilise to give shape and style to our wet- and dry-fly wings.

Fig. 3 shows a pair of wing slips offered to each other, curving inwards to make a wet-fly wing.

Fig. 4 shows the wing slips held firmly between thumb and forefinger and offered to partially formed wet-fly.

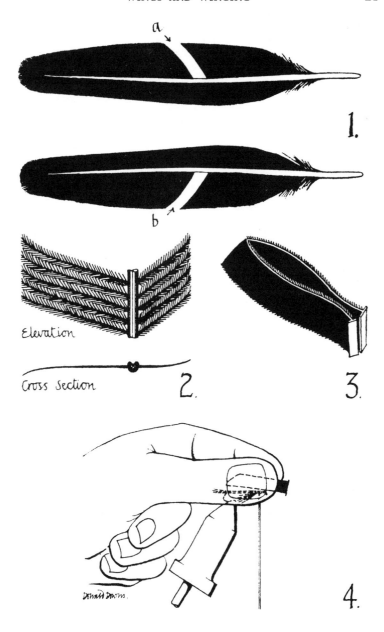

1.

2.

Elevation

Cross Section

3.

4.

Fig. 5 illustrates the all-important "loop over the top" without which it is impossible to achieve a perfectly-formed wing. Silk brought up between *thumb* and feather and then weight of holder used to slip silk down on other side between *finger* tip and feather.

Fig. 6 shows the end elevation of the same stage of procedure, and illustrates clearly how the wing slips, hook-shank, and silk should be confined between the thumb and forefinger.

Fig. 7 shows how the silk is drawn down, still confined between the thumb and forefinger, and Fig. 8 is the end elevation of the same action, and shows how the fibres should be drawn down one on top of the other.

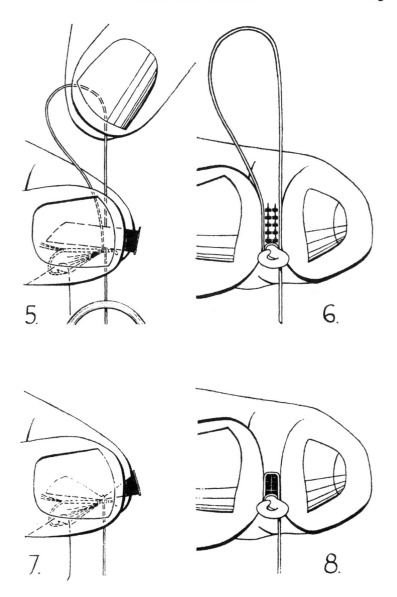

Fig. 9 shows how, after two more turns of silk have been made in the same manner as for Figs. 5–8, the silk can be left held by the weight of a bobbin holder while the waste ends are cut off, using the scissors to make a side cut.

Figs. 10–11 show how the wing butts should taper (this is achieved by using the scissors, so that they come down face-on to the hook-shank and not edge-on), and the finished fly, complete with a whip finish, ready, after varnishing, to go fishing.

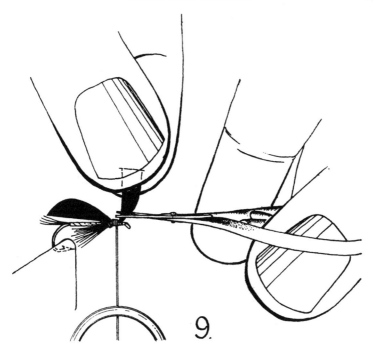

9.

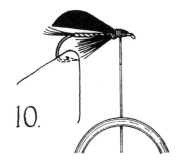

10.

11.

The procedure for tying on dry-fly wings is exactly the same as for wet-fly wings up to the stage where they are left lying horizontally on top of the hook-shank, the main difference being that the two wing slips are offered to each other so that their tips point outwards instead of inwards. This is shown clearly in Fig. 12. The wings are then lifted into the vertical position as per Fig. 13, and two or three turns of the tying silk taken behind them, also as Fig. 13.

Still holding the wings rigidly in the vertical position, another one or two turns should be taken round at the extreme base of the slips as per Fig. 14. This will ensure that the wings stay in the upright position, and this part of the procedure is made easier if one is using a bobbin holder, as this can be "thrown" to the rear of the fly with the right hand, picked up again with the right hand, and wound round the base of the wings. This is necessary as the left hand does not release its hold on the wing-tips during this part of the procedure. Finish off with a final turn round the hook-shank in front of the wings, also as Fig. 14.

The wings can now be released by the left hand and, if they do not part part of their own accord, use the point of the scissors or dubbing needle to separate them.

What we do now is make a "figure-of-eight" turn between the wings, as shown in Figs. 15, 16 and 17, and the fly is now ready for its hackle. It will be observed that a dry-fly hackle is put on *after* the wings, not before, as we did for the wet-fly.

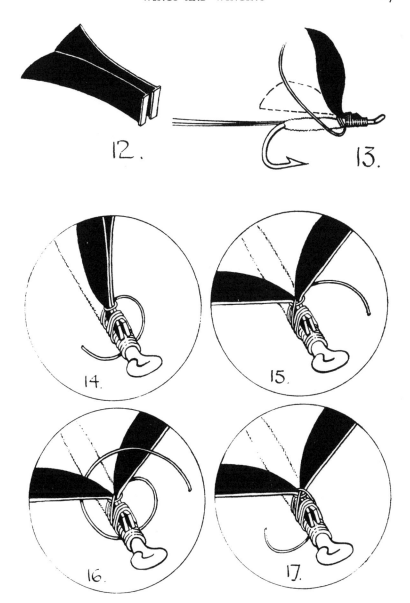

The following method of winging was given to me by Col. D. G. Fraser, and although he states that he has used it for trout flies only, I found it worked just as successfully with salmon fly wings.

The idea is based on the fact that, no matter how carefully wings are compressed and controlled whilst being tied in, there *must* be a tendency for the wing fibres to follow the tying silk over the hook-shank when the silk is drawn tight, and the waxier the tying silk is, the more pronounced becomes the tendency. (Page 16 shows the recognised method of tying in a wing.)

This is very true and, even in a less exaggerated form, it can result in a crease or "pleat" forming on the far side of the wing, although its basic shape may not be affected.

To overcome this one-sided pull, Col. Fraser uses an additional length of tying silk to that being used to tie the fly. This additional length is not waxed, and is used to form the loop over the wing with which we are all familiar, and as *both* its ends can be drawn down at once there is no irregular pull on one side.

To facilitate its introduction between the fingers and over the wing, a small weight is fixed to one end. A light wooden bead is suggested, and the device in use is described as follows:

Normal fly-tying procedure is carried out to the stage where the wings are placed on top of the hook-shank, being held by the forefinger and thumb. The actual tying silk is left hanging down in its holder, or weighted with hackle pliers, at the point where the wing is to be tied in. The beaded end of the unwaxed piece of silk is then inserted plumb-bob-wise between the far side of the hook and the forefinger holding the wing. It is at this stage that the necessity for the weight on the end will be appreciated, as it would be difficult to introduce the silk without some form of weight to control it. A loop is then taken over the extended finger of the free hand, and the other end of the unwaxed silk is guided between the near side of the hook and the thumb holding the wings. The extended forefinger is extracted from the loop, and *both* ends of the unwaxed silk drawn down, compressing the wing fibres on to the top of the hook-shank. Fig. 18 shows an end-on view of the loop over the wings and the two "legs" of the unwaxed silk hanging down. After they have been pulled down, the two "legs" are pushed to the left out of the way, and the actual waxed tying silk is wound round the wings and hook in the normal way. The tips of the finger and thumb can be opened slightly at this stage to ensure that the turns of the tying silk are close up to the point where the loop is holding the wings on the hook-shank. These turns must be to the right of the loop, of course, otherwise the wings will be distorted in the manner described at the beginning of this article.

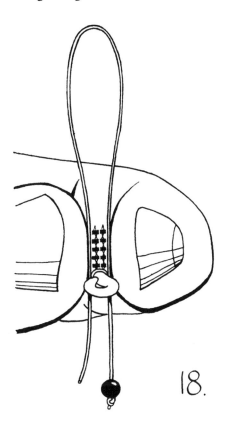

18.

Col. Fraser states that one turn of the tying silk is all that is necessary, and the unwaxed silk is then withdrawn by pulling straight downwards on the beaded end. The surplus wing material can now be cut off and the head of the fly formed. It is always advisable to hold the wings in position while doing this.

I think the idea is an excellent one, so much so that it occurred to me that it might even be improved upon. The most difficult part of the procedure (perhaps "least easy" would be a better description) is the introduction of the unwaxed silk loop between the finger and thumb and over the wing. If the loop could be made rigid, this introduction would be greatly simplified, so I tried replacing the unwaxed silk with a piece of fine but stiffish wire about 6 in. long, and folded in half. It worked first time. The piece of folded wire is held about 1 in. from the bend, Fig. 19, and the introduction of the loop so formed is simplicity itself. The tips of the finger and thumb holding the wing in position are opened slightly, and the loop inserted to the position where the wing is to be drawn down. The finger and thumb are then compressed

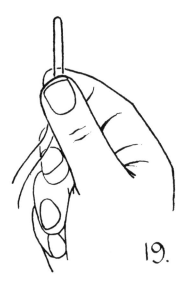

19.

once again, and the piece of wire drawn down as was the beaded silk. The ends of the wire are then pushed to the left and the tying silk brought into play to fix the wing permanently. There is one slight difference in the procedure when using the wire, however. If it was removed, as was the silk, by pulling on one end, it might cut through some of the fibres of the wing. It is better, therefore, to push the loop up slightly from underneath the hook-shank, and then withdraw it from above.

Both these methods produced an absolutely flat wing, seated right on top of the hook-shank, and I hope the many who have had this difficulty with their fly tying will find they are the answer to their problem.

During the course of the articles in the *Fishing Gazette*, a very considerable contribution was made by the late Capt. the Hon. R. Coke, whom I knew for many years as a very keen and meticulous fly-tier.

The following tips of his are concerned with wings and winging, but others will be found in the chapters they concern.

Firstly, his method of winging: the procedure is to carry out the winging process in the usual way, but instead of pulling the loop *down*, the tying silk is taken round the hook-shank underneath, and back between the wing and thumb holding it. The end of the tying silk is then pulled up vertically instead of downwards and as the wing and the hook-shank are totally encompassed by the tying silk, the compression of the wing fibres one on top of the other is assured. The process should be carried out twice and, throughout, the wing and hook-shank must be held firmly in the thumb and forefinger of the left hand, including a small portion of the butt end of the wing. This is most important.

His next tip has to do with our other old friends mallard and teal wings. As you will remember in a previous article, I stipulated that these feathers have more cohesion as wings when double strips of fibres are used for each side of the wing. Capt. Coke's method incorporates the same principle, but it is only necessary to cut off a single strip from each side of the feathers being used, and this is done as follows:

Cut a left- and a right-hand strip from the required feathers, both *double* the width required for the wing, leaving the quills on. Stroke out the fibres to stand at right angles to the quills. Now place the two strips one on top of the other, best side downmost. Now cut the quills off both strips and fold the double strip you now have exactly in half down the middle. A small snip with the scissors at the base of the strips, and in the middle, will help the folding process.

Hold the wing in the forefinger and thumb of the left hand, and if any fibres are out of place they can be removed with a dubbing needle or stiletto. The result is a firm, well-shaped wing ready for tying in, less apt to disintegrate, and having much greater substance.

It is ideal for those flies which require a wing of either teal, mallard, or widgeon, etc., such as the "Teal Blue and Silver", or "Thunder and Lightning". It also eliminates the necessity of tying in an underwing of some other feather when tying a fairly large fly, but if an underwing is part of the dressing, as in a "Blue Charm", for instance, the underwing of mallard can be tied in the normal way, and the overwing of teal folded over it in the manner described in the foregoing. I hope I have made the instructions quite clear, especially as they are not the type which lend themselves easily to illustration.

Although taking the wing slips from the quill is not one of the most difficult tasks facing the fly tyer, it is only by tying many dozens of flies that one acquires the knack of selecting two or more slips of exactly the same width.

To enable every fly tyer to do this, no matter how few winged flies he ties, Mr. W. Weeks, of Sheffield, devised the adjustable preselector illustrated opposite.

This will select wing strips of any size from the narrowest, such as the two-fibred sections required for adding to small "married" salmon fly wings, to the widest, such as the sections for single strip salmon fly and streamer fly wings. In between, of course, it will select strips for all sizes of trout flies, both wet and dry, and also ensure that each pair or pairs of feathers used is an exact match. This may not seem too important, but it is surprising how much better two matched slips tie in than two which are odd sizes.

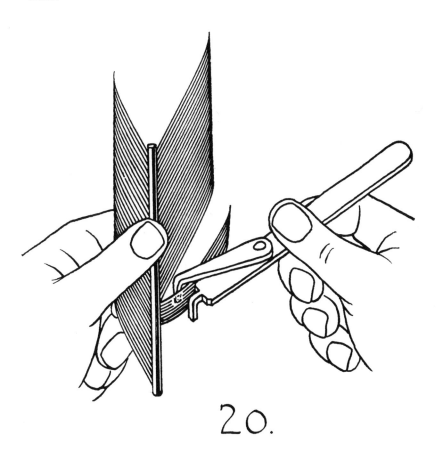

20.

Preparing hen pheasant tails for wings

The ease with which one can prepare materials for wings varies with the type of feather being used. Mallard wing quills are very amenable, whereas the bronze shoulder feathers can be more difficult. It will usually be found that the quill feathers of all birds are always easier to prepare than are the body feathers.

In between the two are the tail feathers used for wings, and of these the hen pheasant tail is about the most difficult to prepare. As they are used very extensively for such flies as the "Invicta" lake- and sea-trout fly, and the low-water salmon fly "March Brown", I think they deserve some special attention.

The usual trouble found is that, no matter how wide a portion of these fibres are cut off, only a very fine tapered wing is produced

This is because of the very acute angle at which the fibres of these tails are set in the quill, and when these fibres are drawn down to stand out at a more usable angle, in the usual manner, they have a strong tendency to spring back to their natural position. This makes it difficult to get a wide portion of fibres to tie in.

To overcome this, I handle the fibres as follows: instead of pulling the fibres right down, I merely separate the required width from the main body of the tail, as Fig. 21. I then grasp the fibres at a point that will make the wing slightly longer than I wish to tie, Fig. 22. I then pull down the fibres remaining on the left very gently, as though the part I was holding with my right hand was the quill. This causes the fibres to take the shape shown in Fig. 23, and I then cut them off where shown (Fig. 24) and tie them in in the usual way (Fig. 24).

I would point out that some of these tails are easier to handle than others, and a good, fresh, long-fibred tail from a mature bird will manipulate much better than a dried-up one, or one from an immature bird. I also find that they tie in much better in the horizontal position than when set upright, although this is not really an important factor.

While on the subject of difficult wing materials, a few words about the mallard shoulder feathers and teal flank feathers would

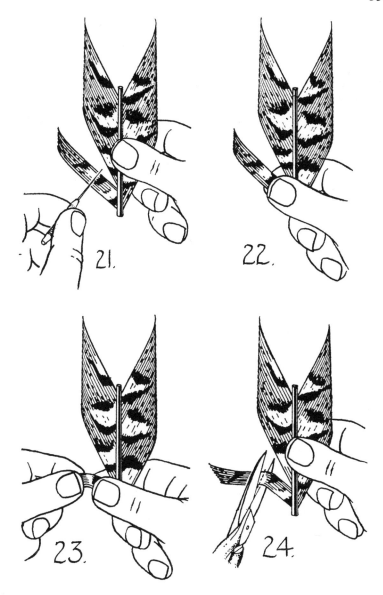

21.

22.

23.

24.

not come amiss. The tips of these feathers have a strong tendency to fly apart when tied in, particularly on small flies.

What should always be remebered about these feathers is that that not only are the main fibres very soft and delicate but also that the intermediary hairs that hold the main fibres together are also delicate in proportion. Consequently, once the fibres are moved or split, they never hold together again quite so well. Therefore, when cutting out the slips, the fibres should not be drawn down as are the fibres on wing quills, they should merely be cut straight off from the feather.

Also, as these soft fibres will compress into a very small space, it is better to make the wings of double thickness. In other words, two slips from a right-hand feather and two slips from a left-hand feather. If these double slips are tied in without disturbing the original shape of the fibres in any way, it will be found that the tendency for their tips to fly apart is greatly reduced. I would also stress once again that one's material should be as fresh as possible, as once the natural oils dry out of these feathers it is almost impossible to keep their tips together when tying in as wings.

With larger flies these difficulties are greatly reduced, the reason for this being that the nearer to the quill of the feather one gets, not only are the fibres much sturdier, they also marry together much better. In fact, an attempt to tie a small fly with the fibres from a large feather will invariably result in the tips flying apart. Unfortunately, it is not possible to get very small brown mallard feathers, as the brown speckling is not present in feathers below a certain size.

In most cases it is far cheaper to buy whole wings if one requires quill feathers for winging purposes, but unless one treats their extraction with a certain amount of circumspection, the important feather fibres on the quills can be damaged enough to make them unusable.

All wings sold for fly tying should be well dried first, not only for the purpose under discussion, but also because this ensures their being free from parasites to some degree. This is carried out by subjecting the wings to a high temperature for several days, so that the fleshy part becomes quite hard and crisp. This process should not be confused with "cooking" over a short period of time, which would make the flesh messy and be harmful to the feather fibres.

To extract the quills from the whole wings, I personally use the following method, which is less harmful to the individual quills than pulling them direct from the flesh:

Grasp the extreme edges of the wing, as Fig. 1.

Give a sharp tug outwards in both directions, so that the wing separates at the base, as Fig. 2.

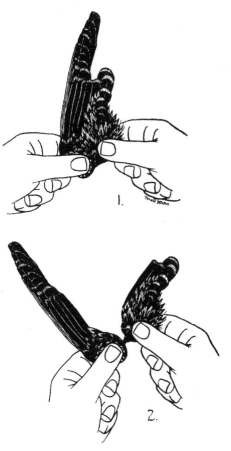

Now take a pair of scissors and cut across the extreme base of the quills on either side, as per Fig. 3.

This will result in all the quills parting cleanly and evenly (Fig. 4), when they should be stored in cellophane envelopes until needed. If you put all the quills from the same pair of wings in each envelope, exact pairing must result.

Some wings, such as mallard, have varied-coloured quills, so in this case the blue coverts would be stored in one envelope and the grey primaries stored in another.

Some wings also supply hackles, so these should be stripped off before the cutting process. I refer to such types as moorhen (under-wing feathers used for "Waterhen Bloa"), grouse and woodcock wing front feathers (used for many wet-fly patterns and spider types), and also another feather from the mallard wings—the underwing white "satins" (used for wet "Coachman"), etc.

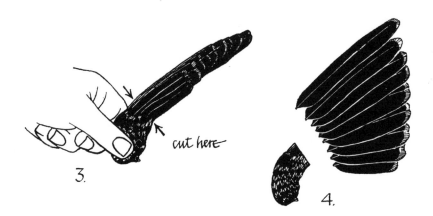

cut here

3.

4.

CHAPTER 2. WINDING HACKLES AND THE WHIP FINISH

The winding of hackles is a frequent item of my correspondence. Doubling them is dealt with in Chapter 3, and this chapter is concerned with the tying and winding of hackles for dry-flies. The usual complaint is as follows:

"When tying hackle dry-flies I find that my flies seem sparse in hackle and untidy compared with shop flies. The hackle fibres seem to point over the eye, rather than give the straight frontal hackle of the professional tyer. Why is this?"

I am often asked this question, and the main answer is that as the professional is always tying flies, his finished product should look better than that of the amateur. This is only a generalisation, of course, as I have seen flies tied by amateurs that were perfect specimens of neatness and balance, and not all the flies one sees in the shops today would get a faultless pass! One result of tying flies continually is the automatic knowledge which is acquired of putting every turn of silk and material in its right place. This is the absolute essence of a well-tied fly.

To concentrate on hackles, however, there are several reasons why the fibres do not stay at an absolute right angle to the hook-shank.

1. If the hackle is not drawn through the fingers so that all the fibres stand out at right angles to the stem, those fibres which are on the side nearest the hook-shank when the hackle is being wound will be splayed out by the stem.

2. Tying in the hackle, so that the fibres are not straight up and down, will result in their going off at different angles when the hackle is wound.

3. If the hackle stem should overlap itself at any time during the winding, the fibres will again be forced out of line.

4. If the hackle is not pulled tight all the time it is being wound, this will result in the stem twisting and sending out the fibres in all directions.

5. Careless winding of the silk through the fibres, if this method of finishing off is used, will also disturb them.

6. Tying in the front fibres when finishing off.

One other point, which you will observe I stress repeatedly in this book: the tying silk must be kept taut at all times when tying flies. Slackness at any time can only result in an untidy-looking fly, or even one that literally falls to pieces before it is removed from the vice.

My method of tying a simple hackle fly is as follows: form tail and body of fly, leaving ample room at the head for hackle. Select the hackle and draw it through the fingers so that it looks like Fig. 2.

Tie it in under or on top of the hook shank, whichever you find comes most naturally to you, holding it by the stem, close to the eye of the hook. The stem should now be at a right angle to the hook-shank, the tip pointing away from you, and the fibres absolutely vertical (Figs. 3 and 4).

Now wind the tying silk back to the body in close, even turns, tying in the stem of the hackle at the same time, which must, of course, be bent back towards the tail for this purpose (Fig. 5).

The turns of silk *must* be even, laid on as they appear on a new reel of silk. Uneven turns of silk will distort the hackle stem. Now grip the tip of the hackle in the hackle pliers and, keeping the hackle taut all the time, wind it up to the body. When the body is reached, allow the hackle tip to hang down in the pliers, and take a turn of silk round it and the hook-shank (Fig. 6). Continue winding the silk through the hackle to the eye of the hook, holding it as tightly as possible. These turns of silk will tie down the hackle stem, and if kept taut it will be observed that the silk hardly disturbs the hackle fibres (Fig. 7). The hackle tip is now cut off.

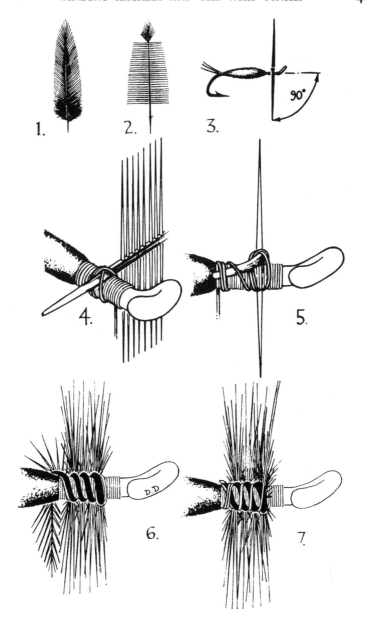

1.

2.

3. 90°

4.

5.

6. D.D

7.

Extra care must be taken when the front fibres are reached, and then two turns are taken in front of them. The fibres should be brushed lightly to the rear before attempting to whip finish in the front, and the turns of this finish should just touch the front fibres, but not overlay them in any way (Figs. 8–12).

I find a whip-finishing tool is invaluable for this, as one can lay the turns of silk in exactly the right place without disturbing the hackle fibres. A symmetrical fly should look like Fig. 13, and if the points I have stressed are fully observed, a result like this is fully guaranteed.

If you possess those very long-stemmed, short-fibred hackles which make the best dry-flies, they can be wound with one side stripped off. This would, of course, be the side nearest the hook-shank when the hackle is wound. Symmetry is assured if this is done, although it must be remembered that the hackle will not be as "full" as when both sides are retained. The foregoing procedure is the same for the stripped hackle also.

With regard to what I said about every turn of silk and material being in its proper place, until this is done automatically it is as well to be able to observe one's flies clearly during the tying. I find the best way to do this is to have one's vice raised up so that the fly is as near to the level of the eyes as possible. It is far better than looking down on the fly. If this cannot be done with your vice, ensure that you have a suitable background so that the fly gives a sharp silhouette. This will show up any slack winding or divergence of the material.

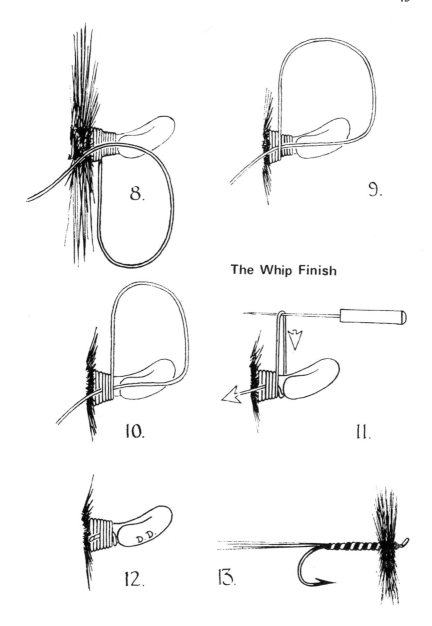

The Whip Finish

8.

9.

10.

11.

12.

13.

CHAPTER 3. DOUBLING HACKLES AND "FALSE" HACKLES

Now for "doubled" hackles. There are several methods of turning back the fibres of hackles, known to us all through various books of instruction, but I will keep to what I think is the most simple one. This entails the use of a spare hook and one's tying vice and hackle pliers.

The hackle to be doubled is tied on to the hook by its tip or butt, and then held vertically by the hackle pliers. The fibres are then stroked to the left, best side outside, until the necessary "V" sectional appearance is attained. It is as simple as that. I advocate doubling the hackles on a spare hook, as if one strokes the fibres a little too vigorously the hackle may be pulled from the hook, and that would be a calamity if it was a body hackle being doubled as the body of the fly would have to be unwound and the hackle tied in afresh. This is not so important, of course, if it is a throat hackle. Also by this method several hackles may be prepared and then put aside until they are required. The illustrations may be of some help: the first, Figs. 1, 2 and 3, showing how the hackle is tied in and treated.

Note that the hackle is tied in close to the body and then wound towards the eye of the hook (Fig. 4).

When winding a body hackle, it is important to ensure that the hackle stalk is not twisted in any way, otherwise the "doubling" is nullified. It also helps if the fibres are stroked back towards the tail during the winding. Make sure that every turn of the hackle is close up against its companion turn of the ribbing tinsel, as this not only protects that hackle stalk, but will also keep the doubled hackle fibres in position (Fig. 5). Fig. 6 shows both doubled body and throat hackles on fly which is now ready for winging.

44

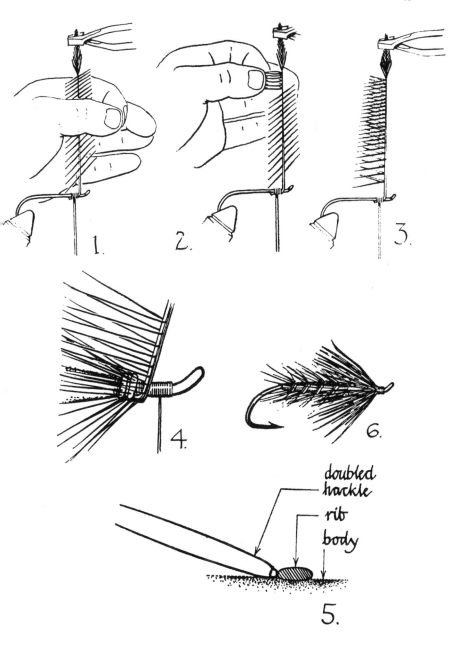

doubled
hackle
rib
body

Another method (Figs. 1–3) of doubling was recently given to me by Jimmy Younger, whose family have been well known in Scottish fly tying and fly fishing for several generations. He uses hackle pliers held in the hand to hold the hackle to be doubled, and the illustration of this method should be clear enough without further explanation from me.

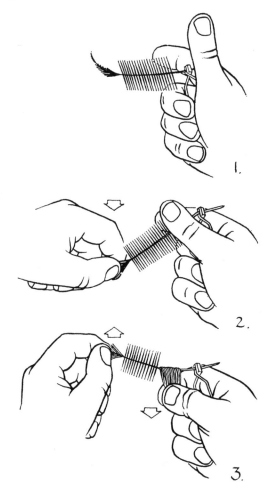

If doubling hackles still presents some difficulty to the reader, the following method of making "false" hackle may produce better results. It is another one of the ideas sent to me by Capt. the Hon. R. Coke, and although it is not a new idea, as he freely admits, he considers it to be one not used generally enough.

"False" hackles consist of a bunch of fibres torn from a feather and tied in at the throat in very much the same manner as one would tie in a wing. By this means, such difficult feathers as blue jay can be used without the bother of splitting the quill and its subsequent breakages, resulting in greater economy and reducing bulk at the head of the fly. Ordinary poultry hackles which are too large for normal use may also be utilised on flies of any size. The procedure is as follows:

The fly is tied to the stage where it is necessary to add the throat hackle, and the tying silk anchored with a half-hitch. The hook is then taken from the vice and put back upside down. The feather to be used as a hackle is then selected, and its fibres pulled down to stand out at right angles to the stem. Tear off a good bunch of the fibres, keeping their tips in line as much as possible. These fibres are now tied in on top of the hook-shank (this is underneath, of course, as the hook is upside down), using the normal winging procedure of the loop over the finger and thumb of the left hand. To spread the fibres over the whole area of the throat it is better to place the fibres rather to the side of the hook facing you, so that when the silk is drawn tight the fibres are pulled over to the far side. In other words, although we are using the winging principle to tie in the fibres, we forget about all the principles we have learned for bringing feather fibres down one on top of the other, but endeavour to produce a split "wing".

After one turn of the tying silk has been taken, it should be put in the retaining button or hackle pliers (if not weighted with a bobbin holder), and the fibres separated and adjusted with a dubbing needle or stiletto. One bunch of fibres is usually enough, but on larger flies another two small bunches can be tied in, one on either side of the original one.

This process may sound involved, but in practice is very simple.

Moreover, when the hook is once again reversed it will be found that there is practically no "hump" to be levelled off before the wings are tied in, which means that a small head results and the wings lie low over the body.

Many feathers can be tied in by this method to give pleasing results other than jay. Partridge body feathers, heron, guinea fowl (gallena) all lend themselves to it, and the necessity of doubling them is eliminated. It can only be applied to throat hackles, of course, as body hackles must still be wound on the stem.

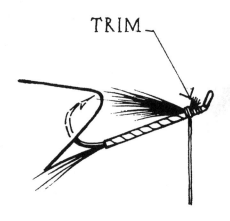

TRIM

"FALSE" HACKLE

CHAPTER 4. STIFFENING DRY-FLY HACKLES & HACKLING DAPPING FLIES

Still on the subject of hackles, Capt. Coke had the following method of stiffening his dry-fly hackles, an idea born of the scarcity of the good quality hackles required to keep our flies afloat. It is this: after completing the fly to the stage where the hackle is required, select a large hackle of the same colour and cut off about 1 in. from the tip. This is the best part to use, as any web which may be in the feather is much less apparent at its extreme tip. Stroke the fibres to right angles to the stem and clip them to about $\frac{1}{8}$ in. in length either side of the stem. The length would vary according to the size of fly, of course, but in this instance we are left with a hackle 1 in. long with a width of $\frac{1}{4}$ in. along its entire length.

This hackle is now tied in at the shoulder of the fly, and one, or at the most two, turns taken round the hook-shank and finished off. The effective hackle is then selected and tied in and wound behind and in front of the cut hackle, and the fly finished off in the usual way.

The stiff, short fibres of the cut hackle act as stiffeners to the weaker fibres of the ordinary hackle, and are quite invisible if the job is done properly. A fly tied in this manner is most effective in rough water, where it is most important to have one which cocks and floats well.

Incidentally, this two-hackle principle is used for the Dr. Baigent "Refracta" dry-flies, the difference being that instead of the long-fibred hackle being cut short it is left long, the effective hackle forming the legs forming the centre of the hackle. By this means, Dr. Baigent claimed that the surface of the water was disturbed by the fibres of the long hackle, giving an altered refraction

49

and thus a more natural look to the artificial from the fish's point of view.

The heavy hackling required to float dapping flies, through the air as well as on the surface of the water, require little explanation so I have provided no drawings for this. One uses the same method as shown in chapter 2 "Winding Hackles", the only difference being that instead of one single hackle being tied in and wound, two or three are tied in together and wound at the same time as though they were a single hackle. This produces the thick "bushy" effect which is the main characteristic of dapping flies.

CHAPTER 5. MAKING FLIES WITH "PARACHUTE" HACKLES

The popularity and demand for the "parachute" hackled fly is universal, for I have had requests from overseas as well as the British Isles as to the best method of making them up. There are many reasons why this type of fly is so popular, namely:

1. It lands on the water surface in a much more natural manner, due of course to the parachute effect of the horizontally wound hackle.

2. Once on the water the fly is almost unsinkable, due to the greater amount of hackle fibre on which it rests.

3. The spread of hackle is better arranged to support the fly in the correct position on the water, and so makes a better representation of the natural fly.

As most of you will already know, parachute flies differ from flies tied in the orthodox manner in that the hackle is wound on a horizontal plane, not on a vertical one as is usual. To facilitate this, a vertical projection on top of the hook-shank is required, but hooks already fitted with this projection are not readily available. Consequently tyers have resorted to many makeshifts in order to overcome this difficulty, such as whipping pieces of wire or bristle to the top of the hook-shank, with a projecting end bent upwards. Another method uses the hackle stalk itself, but the drawback with this method, as with most of the others, was the lack of rigidity in the projection during the actual tying. It was possible to produce flies by these methods, but the results in most cases were far from satisfactory as far as appearance and durability were concerned.

The making of "parachutes" became a subject I preferred to avoid, until I had the good fortune to receive a visit from Bob

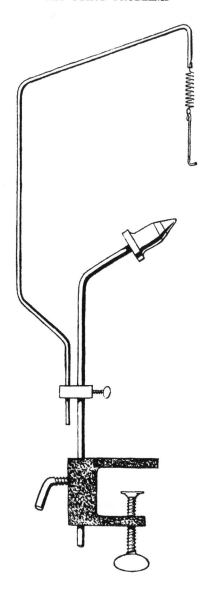

Barlow while he was over here on holiday from Australia. He is an Englishman engaged as an engineer at the Woomera research station, and his obvious brilliance in the particular sphere has, fortunately for us, also expressed itself in his fly-tying activities.

His fly-tying kit is a revelation of ingenuity—magnetic-based vices, multiple-range hackle guards, moulds for reproducing realistic nymph and larvae imitations, and, most interesting of all as far as I was concerned, a "gallows" to facilitate the making of the parachute fly.

He very kindly gave us permission to produce this "gallows" in our own way, and our tool engineer came up with the device illustrated. Like all good ideas, it is a simple one, and although it uses the hackle-stalk loop method I mentioned previously, it enables the loop to be kept rigid enough to make the hackle winding as easy as that round the hook-shank in the orthodox manner. In fact it is so easy that when I came to make up the hackle-point wing example illustrated and described here, I found I could produce them quicker than those I make in the conventional style!

Illustration No. 3 shows how the hook on the spring keeps the loop firm enough for the hackle to be wound. When the winding is finished, pointed-nose tweezers are inserted into the loop and the tip of the hackle pulled through. The spring-loaded hook is then released (most important) and the tip of the hackle and its stalk are then pulled as one would pull the two ends of a knot. In fact, by this method, the hackle is virtually tied in a knot. The pulling of the hackle stalk, while holding the tip of the hackle in the tweezers or fingers, draws the loop down on the end of the hackle, and this not only ensures a firm and durable fixture but also obviates the necessity of adding clear varnish to the centre as is often required by other methods. I prefer to hold the hackle tip in my fingers when the stalk is being pulled, as there is less possibility of the hackle tip being broken off. This is of course important if the hackle tip is to be left on to form a wing.

Personally I prefer to leave the hackle tips on all the patterns I make for myself, and in fact I use two hackles at a time because

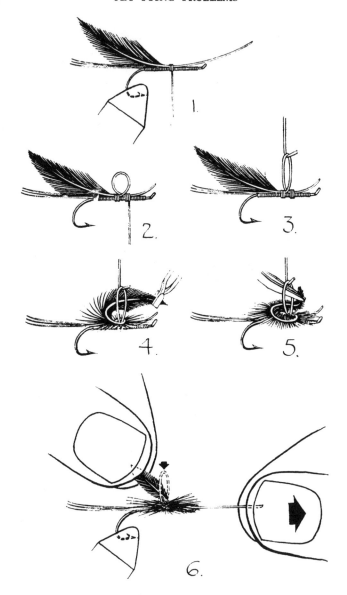

of this. The method is exactly the same, but I discovered that the finished articles were some of the most lifelike and durable dry-flies I have ever produced.

I now come to what in my mind is the most important aspect of our now being able to tie parachute flies with such simplicity. As we all know, the biggest problem facing the tyer of dry-flies is the increasing scarcity of good small hackles of superior quality required for this purpose. The mere fact of making ones flies as "parachutes" resolves this difficulty automatically. This, of course, requires some further explanation, but it is quite simple: The best hackle or hackles to use for making parachute flies are those of a medium to large size, and which are web-free at the tips. Only the last half inch to three-quarters have to be used, and as even poor quality cock hackles in these sizes are invariably web-free at this part, the oft-repeated search for a good stiff web-free hackle for a dry-fly is no longer necessary! I do not doubt that there is not a fly-tyer in the country who does not have many dozens of hackles or parts of hackle capes that he considered were unusable for dry-fly work. This must be particularly so where the black-centred type of hackle is concerned (Greenwell, Coch-y-bonddu, Badger, etc.), as the black centre marking is always more predominant in the larger feathers, I do not think I have to enlarge further on this side of the matter, except to say that I think this can be regarded as a major break-through as far as the shortage of dry-fly hackles problem is concerned.

The next aspect we come to is making use of the fact that the procedure results in the hackle or hackles being tied in a knot. Because of this it is possible to cut through the turns of tying silk underneath the hook-shank, and remove the parachute in its entirety—complete with hackle stalks and wings. The hackle stalks can then be used as tail whisks and threaded through a plastic fly body so that we then not only have a parachute fly, but a detached-body representation also.

The first illustration shows the "gallows" fixed to the vice, and as this is a universal fixture it should fit most gauges of vice stem. The rest of the procedure, with illustrations, is as follows:

Fig. 1. The hackle, with at least two-thirds or three-quarters of its length stripped, is laid on top of the hook-shank. Tails and body should be put on first, of course. If one finds it easier to work with the hackle the other way round, i.e., with the stalk over the bend of the hook, this is quite all right. One uses the method one finds easiest.

The hackle stalk is now looped round and the butt tied down again. One should endeavour to do this so that a perfect circle is obtained without any gap at the base. Two or three turns of silk should be sufficient for this, but one must ensure that a bobbin holder is used or that the end of the tying silk is held firmly in "catch", otherwise the spring-loaded hook could pull the hackle-stalk loop out of its moorings (Fig. 2).

Fig. 3 shows the spring-loaded hook in place, and Fig. 4 the hackle being wound round the loop.

After several turns have been made round the loop, the tweezers are inserted through the loop and the hackle gripped as shown in Fig. 5. The tip of the hackle is then drawn through the loop, and the stalk then drawn tight to form the "knot" as shown in Fig. 6. As this action is illustrated in "broken line", the unbroken part of the illustration clearly shows the completed parachute effect.

Figs. 8 and 9 show two hackles being used and the resulting hackle-point wing effect, with parachute.

On reaching this stage it is now possible to cut the "knotted" hackle from the hook with a razor blade, Fig. 10, and Figs. 11-12-13 shows their adaptation to the detached body and the resulting detached-body fly.

All the illustrations show the stages being carried out on an up-eyed hook, but it is quite in order to use a down-eyed hook for this type of dry-fly. The down-eyed hook has the advantage of the eye being out of the way during the tying procedures, and it also makes the job of tying the fly to the cast a little easier.

It is my considered opinion that with this simple gadget Bob Barlow has made a really considerable contribution to fly tying, not only by solving the problem of making parachute flies easily, but also by overcoming the nagging problem known to all dry-fly tyers—the shortage of good hackles for this purpose.

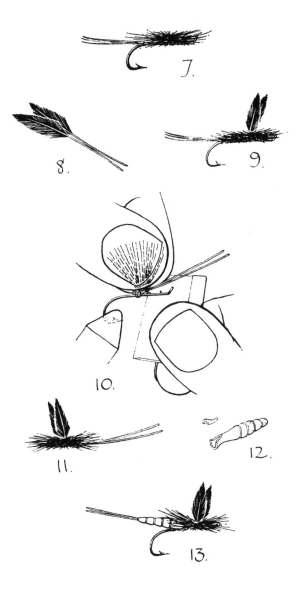

CHAPTER 6. STRIPPING PEACOCK HERLS FOR QUILL BODIES

The "herls" that go to make up the actual bright-coloured "eye" part of the peacock tail deserve special mention. When stripped of their flue they have a double colour, the part from which the flue is stripped being brown, and the remainder of the quill being a lighter colour of beige or grey. The lightness of this colour varies in the quills, and the "eyes" should be inspected at the back to ensure that they are light in colour. When wound round the hook-shank, this double-marked quill gives a very life-like imitation of the rib markings of many natural insects, and forms the body material of well-known patterns such as the "Red Quill", "Blue Upright", "Rusty Variant", "Ginger Quill", etc. The quills need to be dyed for some of these patterns. The double-marked quills from the "eye" tail start at the greenish-yellow triangle at the base of the "eye". All the quills below this point are one colour only.

The quills are very delicate and unless treated with care will break very easily.

One method of stripping them is as follows:

Hold the quill in the left forefinger and thumb, leaving about half an inch of the root end projecting to the right. Now scrape it from A–B between the right thumb-nail and the ball of the right forefinger, and at intervals, between the right forefinger nail and the ball of the right thumb. This will ensure that both sides of the quill are treated in the same manner. Extend the quill to the right a little more, and carry out the same process until about 1 inch has been cleaned. This will be sufficient for bodies on hooks up to size 12 (3).

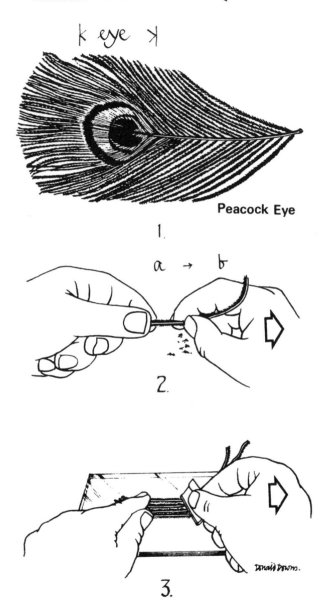

Peacock Eye

1.

2.

3.

Another method which may be found more satisfactory is as follows:

Place the quill on a small sheet of glass or any other smooth or glossy surface, and hold it in position with the left forefinger. An old razor blade is now used for the scaping, and the quill must be turned over so that both sides are cleaned. The blade should slope slightly to the right, so that its edge does not bite into the quill and split it (Fig. 3).

The second method will be found the quicker of the two, although the finger-nail may have to be brought into play for any odd fibre that proves stubborn.

There are always many breakages when one starts to strip pea-cock quills, but they become less as one's experience increases. The thing to remember is not to strip too much at a time, and this applies more to the finger-nail method than it does to the razor-blade method. More than one quill can be scraped at a time as shown in Fig. 3.

Another method, and a very good one, is to use a pencil rubber instead of the razor blade. The heavy, soft type of rubber used by artists and draughtsmen is the best.

I was taken to task, and rightly so, for not mentioning this in the Forum article which dealt with the subject.

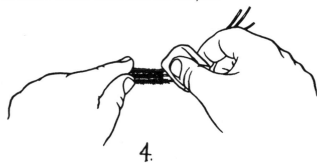

4.

CHAPTER 7. RARE HACKLES, SUPPLY, DEMAND AND SUBSTITUTES

The subject of hackles, particularly those for dry-flies, is continually cropping up in my correspondence, not so much regarding the tying of them, but how to obtain certain types which are very scarce. To understand the problem fully, it is necessary to know the circumstances affecting supply, and the reasons for the shortage of some kinds.

In the first place, some of the more popular types are freaks, which means that birds cannot be bred to guarantee a certain type of hackle. Within this range of types we have the furnace hackles required for the popular "Greenwell's Glory", red/black for "Coch-y-Bondhu", and badger for "Grey Duster" and other flies. All these have one common feature, a black centre, and sometimes the tips of the hackles are also black. They are the outcome of crossing various strains of birds, usually by the introduction of game breeds into the flocks.

The main strains concentrated on by breeders for best egg- and flesh-producing results, are Red and Light Sussex, the Blacks and any other strains being introduced to improve the breed. The resulting birds, therefore, are nearly all Reds or Light Sussex, with now and again the improving breed cropping up in the plumage. A good furnace or a good badger may crop up only once in several thousand birds, which is the reason for the small number of required types, compared with the many hundreds of plain colours.

While breeders concentrate on these, to them, more profitable types, the number of freaks must continue to grow less. Added to this is the fact that many of the old breeds are no longer encouraged, which is the reason that Plymouth Rock (grizzle) hackles are now as scarce as were the coveted Andalusian types from which we obtained our Blue Duns, Iron Blues, Honey Duns, etc. This breed is now practically extinct.

Although there must be many birds killed every year, which would supply us with the hackles we require, modern methods of storing (cold store) and machinery plucking, render the hackles useless to the fly tyer. Many of them would be useless anyway, as few birds are allowed to reach the maturity that produces the hard hackles so necessary for the dry-fly.

With the greatly increased production of table birds, it might be thought that there were plenty of hackles made available to the fly tyer, but unfortunately this is not the case at all. The modern system of producing "broilers" results in birds covered by nothing but a stubbly brown, absolutely useless for our purposes.

Before the war, the British poultry market supplied practically all the hackles we used, but the above-mentioned conditions have reduced this source of supply to a mere trickle. We also obtained many from what are now known as Iron Curtain countries, and even if these became available once again, no doubt we would find that they also have adopted the new methods of plucking and storing.

Consequently, new sources of supply had to be found, and the majority of our hackles now come from the East. Although quite a large number of the capes of hackles received from this source are excellent for dry-flies, the range of types is very limited for the same reasons as I have expounded at the beginning of this chapter. We must count our blessings, however, because if it were not for this source of supply there would not be enough good hackles of any kind to go round, and those available would be almost priceless. We can but hope that the aforementioned modern methods will not reach that part of the world for some time. Even now, it is becoming more noticeable that the strains are getting more concentrated, and the number of "freaks" growing smaller.

In an effort to overcome some of these shortages, dyed substitutes are taking the place of the Andalusian types, but it is, of course, impossible to dye a badger, and there are not enough badgers to spare for dyeing furnace.

The only ways to overcome the shortage of the freak hackles are: 1, use larger hackles; 2, cut hackles; or 3, resort to a substitute which I described in the *Fishing Gazette* several years ago. It is almost impossible to tell that the resulting fly has not been tied with a black-centred hackle, and although I know that the idea does not meet with the approval of purists, I can but say, "What else are we to do?"

My idea sprang from the method I had seen used by several fly tyers, amateur and professional, which incorporated a small, short-fibred black hackle with a red, white or ginger hackle, the black hackle being used, of course, to simulate the black centre. I replaced the black hackle with a strand of ostrich herl, and found it most effective. If one wishes to tie a "Greenwell" the method is as follows:

Form body with rib—with a tail if required, leaving plenty of room at the eye end of the hook. Tie in the strand of ostrich herl close up to the body and continue winding the silk until the eye is nearly reached. Tie in the ginger hackle and wind the silk back to the ostrich herl. Wind the hackle up to the ostrich herl, tie in its tip and cut off the surplus. Wind the tying silk back through the hackle to the eye. Now wind the herl through the hackle to the eye, holding it as taut as possible so that the hackle fibres are not disturbed too much. When the eye is reached, tie in the herl and cut off the surplus. Finish off fly with the usual whip finish.

The amount of black centre is, of course, governed by the number of turns given to the herl, and we found that for a lightly dressed fly, one turn at the back of the hackle, one or two through the hackle, and one in the front were all that was necessary.

Flies requiring a badger or a furnace hackle are tied in the same manner, using a white or a red hackle.

Winged dry-flies can also be tied, the wings being put on before the hackle and herl.

Wet-flies are treated in the same manner, by using hen hackles, or soft cock hackles.

Artificial colouring of hackles has also been tried, but this was always a difficult task for the black centred hackles, although some fair results were achieved with barred ones. This was done by sealing off parts of the hackles so that the dye only affected the exposed parts, but results were far from natural looking, and any dye seeping into the sealed off parts ruined the whole effect or just produced a mess.

The method I am going to describe here has none of these drawbacks, and produces the most natural looking artificially coloured hackles I have ever seen! Flies I have tied would defy any attempts to say that they were made other than with natural marked hackles, the artificial colouring is waterproof and, as far as I have been able to ascertain to date, the spirit base of the colouring used seems to enhance the quality of the hackle. This seems to be due to the fact that the usually absorbant centre web of the hackle soaks up most of the spirit colouring, thus becoming waterproof itself. In addition, the colours are so fast that I have been unable to make them run even when washed in hot water a few minutes after they have been processed.

To sum up, it seems to me that we have at leaest made quite a break-through in the solving of the rarer hackle shortage.

I have no wish to take the credit for the discovery; all I have done is to give it a thorough testing and ascertain its potential in various directions. I was started off along these lines by Geoffry Bucknall, who very kindly passed the idea on to me to develop and publicise it as I saw fit. He first thought of the artificial colouring of feathers, etc., when he discovered that a felt-tipped pen was ideal for "dyeing" stripped peacock quills used for quill-bodied flies. A quick run up and down the exposed side of the quill after stripping, and before tying in, of course, was all that was necessary, and it was this attribute that made him suggest to me that it could be a useful idea for artificially marking hackles. What I had to do was merely to evolve a method of procedure which would produce an even and natural looking bar or stripe, whichever was required, and in the quickest possible time. I also had to decide which type of felt-tipped pen was best for the job.

There are several kinds of these pens on the market, and the one I found most useful is the stubby "Magic Marker", which has a rather broad, square tip cut obliquely. This enables one to make either a fine or heavy mark, which is very useful when making stripes which are broad at the base of the hackle and fine at the tip.

The fine, round-tipped, long felt pens are also quite useful, particularly when marking very small hackles, but they are not quite so profuse in dispensing the waterproof ink.

Before starting to mark the hackles there are two important points to remember. (a) Hackles requiring a centre stripe should have the fibres down to right angles to the stem as per Fig. 1. (b) Those to be used for cross-barring should be left in the natural position, Fig. 2.

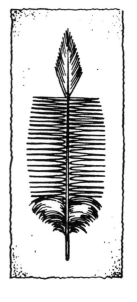 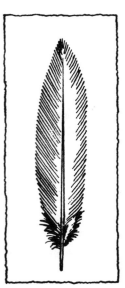

1   2.

To ensure good penetration of the colour, always work on an absorbent surface—blotting-paper for instance, or old newspaper.

To achieve a neat straight edge to the centre bar, use a straight-edge ruler (wood or metal), aligned to taper as Fig. 3.

The colouring is applied by a series of dots, any gaps being filled in by further dotting. Trying to draw a line along the hackle only drags the hackle fibres, and the result is an uneven edge to the centre line Fig. 4 gives some idea of how the hackle should look on completion.

If the centre stripe is not as dark as you would like, turn the hackle over and repeat the process on the back. This is one way we can improve on nature, as all natural hackles are lighter on the back than at the front. In fact, this "chalkiness" has always been a drawback on naturals.

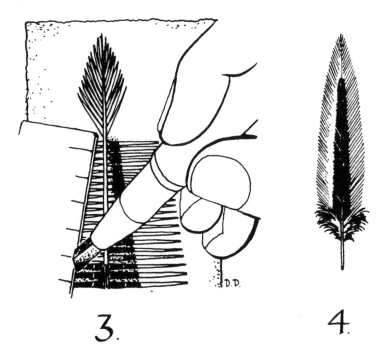

3. 4.

If a black tip is required on the edges of the fibres (the true Coch-y-bonddu marking), the straight edge should cover the whole of the hackle except the extreme tips, and the tips "dotted" as described above.

A cross-barred hackle such as a Grizzle is produced in the same manner, using the undisturbed hackle as described above, but dotting them horizontally, of course. These hackles should also be turned over if a darker effect is required, and slightly heavier dotting at the centre of each bar, where the fibres meet the stem, produces a very natural effect. In fact, flies tied with these hackles have been passed as "naturals" by experienced members of our staff who have spent many years handling hackles of every colour and quality (Figs. 5 and 6).

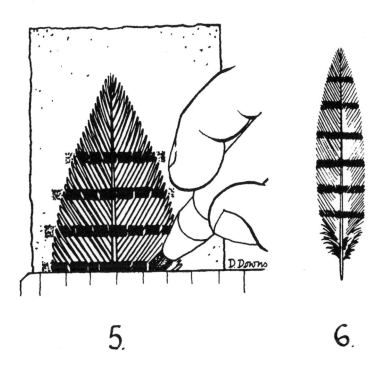

5.   6.

I know there are many who will still prefer to use the natural coloured hackles and insist that it is not possible to improve on nature. This may be partly true, but I think that the ideas I have expounded here are as near as we are likely to get artificially, and when it comes to quantity, this is only limited by the number of plain coloured hackles that need to be transformed. There is no shortage of reds, light or dark, for producing Greenwell's and Coch-y-bonddus, and it is rarely that one is unable to obtain white hackles either loose or in cape form for Grizzle or Badger.

With regard to time, I have estimated that it takes about the same time to mark one side of a hackle as it does to strip the flue from a peacock herl when making quill-bodied flies. It varies, of course, according to the size of hackle being marked.

One final comment. The method does not have to be restricted to the special hackles I have mentioned, but could also be applied to hackles of every hue and for many different purposes. In fact a very good small streamer fly imitation of a Perch fry was obtained by tying two dark ginger hackles alongside the shank, after they had been cross-barred as for making a Grizzle hackle. The result was most natural, and in this case the result was better than using the natural "Cree" hackle one would normally think of for this purpose.

As this immediately starts one thinking about "Badger Duns", "Grizzle Duns", and other possibilities by artificial colouring, the enormous scope of this new method will be more readily grasped.

Try it for yourself and see!

The only "snag" we have come up against so far, is that although the marking ink is waterproof, floatants of the "Mucilin" type can cause the colour to run. To overcome this I first treat my hackles with the floatant, allow them to dry, and then carry out the marking. When they flies are finished I apply more floatant using an aerosol type of applicator, and by this means have been able to retain all the colour with only imperceptible effect from the floatant. If one uses good quality hackles the less floatant one needs of course.

CHAPTER 8. MAKING "SHAVING-BRUSH" FLIES

The most straightforward method I have found for forming the wings of these flies is as follows: *Hackle Wings:* use a very stiff hackle with good length to the fibres—a saddle hackle is the best if one can obtain them. Draw the hackle through the fingers so that the fibres stand out at right angles to the stem as Fig. 1. Tear off about $\frac{1}{4}$ to $\frac{1}{2}$ in. of fibres as is shown at the bottom of the illustration, and it is most important that the tips of the fibres be kept level. These should be tied in on top of the hook-shank as per Fig. 2, a layer of tying silk being put on first so that the fibres will not twist round the shank. This will not be sufficient for the "wings" and there should be two or three lots of fibres tied in. I advocate the tearing of only a few of the fibres as a time, otherwise it is difficult to keep the tips in line.

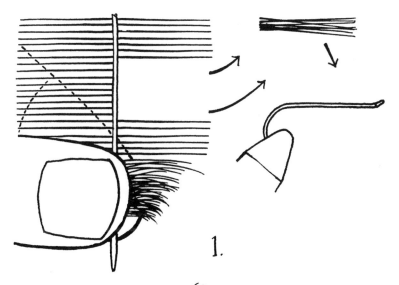

1.

Two or three turns of the tying silk must be put round the hook-shank and the fibres to ensure that they are well anchored, and then a half-hitch to fasten the silk. The fibres must now be parted in the centre and pressed to stand out at an angle on each side of the hook-shank, and turns of the tying silk taken between them and round the hook-shank as shown in enlarged form in Fig. 3. This also shows how the wings should appear as seen from above.

The tail body and rib are now formed, and the hackle wound over the base of the wings to cover the turns of silk used to fix them in position. The finished fly should now be as Fig. 4. Why it is called a "Shaving Brush" immediately becomes obvious.

Fur Wings: the method of tying in these wings is very similar, but it is even more important that a good bed of tying silk be wound on to the hook-shank before the fibres are tied in. Fur fibres are very prone to twist round the hook-shank when the silk is pulled tight unless this is carried out.

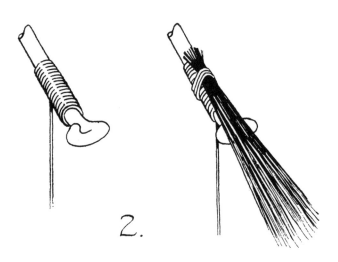

2.

To cut the fibres from the skin, raise up a bunch and twist them. If the diameter of the twisted fibres is about $\frac{1}{8}$ in., this will be sufficient for a May-fly, less being required for small flies. Cut the fibres off near to the skin, making sure that their tips remain in line as for the hackle fibres. The fur fibres are now tied in on top of the hook-shank, and fixed with a half-hitch as before. Now cut off the surplus ends of the fibres, as they will only get in the way at this stage. The fibres must now be lifted up and two turns of the tying silk put round them alone, and then a further two round them and the hook-shank as per Fig. 5. This will anchor them firmly, as this springy material has a habit of working loose unless well tied in. It is as well to put a drop of cellire varnish on the turns of silk at this stage to make them really secure. The fur fibres must now be separated and fixed in this position as were the hackle fibres, and the fly completed by adding the tail, body, rib and hackle. The appearance of the "Wulff" in silhouette is the same as the "Shaving Brush", but I prefer the former for its floating qualities.

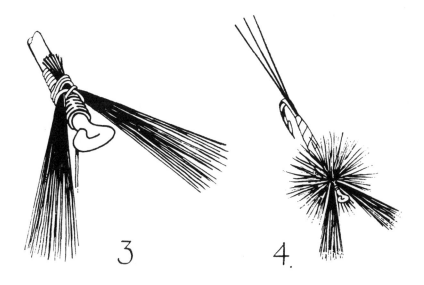

The two main points to remember are:

1. A good bed of silk on which to tie the fibres, especially for the bucktail ones.

2. Leave plenty of room at the eye end of the hook for manipulation of the wings during tying, and also for when the time comes to attach the cast to the fly.

As a result of the article on the "Shaving Brush" type of fly, I received another method of forming these wings from Mr. K. Stewart, of Stevenston, Ayrshire.

By his method the wings are tied beforehand, to be affixed to the fly at the appropriate stage. His method is as follows:

A pin is bent to the shape of a hook and placed in the vice (I found that a tapered-shank hook was also effective), and then two good quality, stiff-fibred hackles are tied in and wound to the right, as one would do on a normal fly. The fingers are then moistened and the fibres stroked to the right, as shown in Fig. 6. They must be pulled firmly to get them into this position. Now take a separate piece of waxed tying silk and wind two or three turns at the point shown in Fig. 7. Tie them very tightly, and add a slight touch of clear varnish to the binding. The fibres are now cut through at the point also shown in Fig. 7, and the wing is then ready to be added to the fly being tied. Any number of these "wings" can, of course, be made up before starting on the flies proper, but time must be allowed for the varnish to dry before using them.

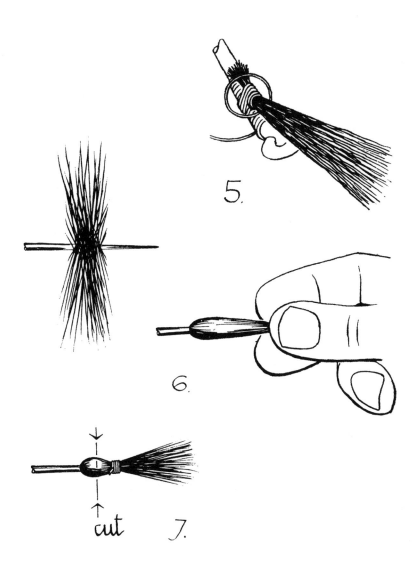

5.

6.

cut   7.

To be a good fly tyer, one must not only know how to tie the materials on to the hook, it is also necessary to know how to take advantage of their characteristics. The natural curve of the fibres on a wing quill, for instance, can be utilised to give a desired curve to the wing being made from them.

The herls used for bodies or butts also have a helpful characteristic in that the fibres on the quills run along one edge only. If a quill is cut across, looking at the two ends produced one sees the cross section as illustrated below.

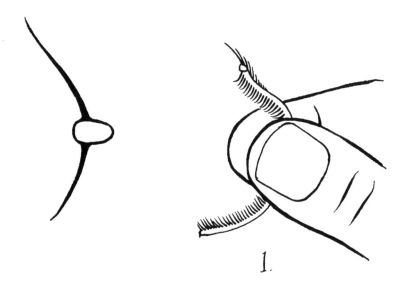

1.

The peacock and ostrich herls, which are used so extensively in fly tying, have this characteristic very markedly, and by taking advantage of this a neat, well-shaped tag can be put on a salmon fly, and a good, full body on a trout fly.

For the butt, the ostrich herl should be tied in underneath the hook-shank and on the extreme right of the space devoted to the butt, with the fibres on the left-hand side, Fig. .2 The herl is then wound once to the extreme left, as per Fig. 2, and the remaining turns made to the right so as to cover this first turn, as Fig. 3 & 4. I do not think this requires further clarification, and you will find that it always produces good results. (Fig. 4).

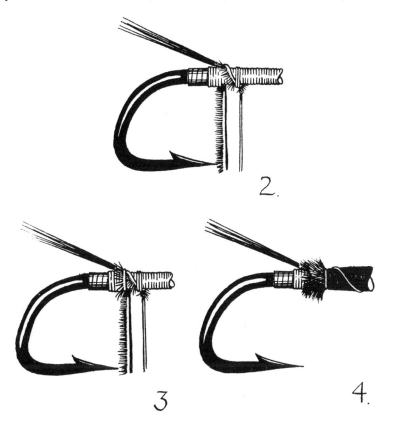

2.

3

4.

For a trout-fly body, I always use two strands of peacock herl tied in together at the tail end of the fly, both having the fibres or "flue" on the left-hand side. The two quills are now wound one after the other, each turn of the rearmost quill being brought down on to the top of the foremost one, as shown in Fig. 5. This produces a much fuller body than if the two quills are twisted together, as is advocated in some fly-tying books.

I have also been asked how to avoid the gap which often appears between one of these herl bodies and its hackle. To do this, the hackle should be tied in at the eye of the hook, and not close up to the body. The tying silk is then wound back to the body, followed by the hackle, which must be wound right up to the herl body. The tying silk is then wound back to the eye, through the hackle, and tied off. This method eliminates the gap and also ensures a firm fixture of the hackle.

When selecting herls for tags or bodies, it is, of course, necessary to choose those which have plenty of "flue" on them. This varies considerably, and the selection should be made according to the size of the fly being tied.

CHAPTER 10. *PREPARING AND TYING IN GOLDEN PHEASANT CRESTS FOR TOPPINGS AND TAILS*

Although salmon flies take longer to tie than trout flies, in my opinion they are much easier, and they do not present so many difficulties to the amateur. The two main items of procedure that most beginners find difficult to overcome are: (1) putting on the final topping of golden pheasant crest; and (2) doubling the body and throat hackles.

It is these two items for which I get most requests for advice and assistance. Both have something in common in that if the feathers are prepared properly before they are tied in the difficulties are reduced. I will deal with the golden pheasant crest here, doubling hackles being dealt with in Chapter 3.

These feathers, when on the living bird, are a perfect shape for putting on a salmon fly, but during the drying and storing of the skins many of the crests get twisted out of shape. It is logical to assume, therefore, that if one form of treatment will put the feathers out of shape, another will restore them to a useful contour once again.

Moistening them and placing them in the curve of wine glasses, etc., is one method frequently advocated, but this rather limits the shapes one can attain and does not always remove the twist. The best method I know is to moisten them thoroughly and then lay them on their sides on a smooth surface in the shape you wish them to attain. I use a part of a linoleum work-bench myself, and, provided one knows that the feathers are clean, saliva is the best moistener.

The feathers must be made very wet, and the shape required is imparted by the finger-tips. Any shape can be achieved, from a dead straight line to a half-circle, or the end of the crest can be

77

turned down sharply so that it curves down to meet the tail of the fly in a pleasing manner.

The crests should be left on the flat surface until they are quite dry, otherwise the desired shape is not maintained. On removal it will be observed that all the fibres of the crest are clinging together, and to bring it back to its natural state I use a stiffish fibred brush of the type normally used to clean typewriter keys. This brushing will not remove the imparted shape, especially if the crests are allowed to stand for a good length of time before being picked up. I like to leave mine for twenty-four hours.

The next step is to remove the unwanted fibres from the butt end of the crest, leaving it the required length of the fly to be tied. The stripped butt is then flattened between the thumbnail and the ball of the first finger, and one will find that its soaking has made the quill more amenable to this treatment.

One very good aspect of this method is the fact that as the crest has lain on its side during the shaping process, the curve is always in an exactly flat plane with all twist removed. Therefore, when it is placed over the wing, the flattened quill can be tied in at once, without it being necessary to manipulate it, so that the crest will envelope the wing properly.

It is always a good idea to select a crest about $\frac{1}{2}$ in. longer than the wing to be covered, as this makes it easier for the stripped and flattened butt to be tied in.

Crests for tails can also be treated in the same manner, again using a longer one than is strictly necessary, so that only the butt is tied in and none of the fibres. This prevents the latter splaying out in all directions.

The foregoing instructions may seem rather long drawn out, but the actual procedure will be found to be very simple and will impart that extra "finish" which is the hallmark of a well-tied fly.

CHAPTER 11. MAKING "DUBBING" BODIES

I was shown the following method by a professional tyer who gave me my first instruction in tying many years ago, and I have yet to see any superior method either for quickness of application or durability in use.

You all must have seen illustrations of dubbing spiralled round the tying silk, but this is not good enough if the fur is to stay on during use. It must encompass the tying silk completely, as does the rubber casing round a piece of electric wire.

Important points to remember during the spinning of the fur on to the silk are:

1. See that the tying silk is well waxed.

2. Only use a small amount of fur at a time, spread out to cover as large an area of the thumb as possible.

3. Do *not* roll the silk backwards and forwards on the thumb, but in *one* direction only.

4. Keep the tying silk taut all the time.

The procedure is as follows: hold the tying silk taut in the right hand, at a right angle to the hook and pulling it towards the body. Select a minute pinch of the necessary fur and spread it on the ball of the left forefinger or thumb, whichever you find easiest. If it looks more like an almost indiscernible mist rather than a bunch of fur fibres, so much the better, especially for small trout flies. Now bring the taut silk down on the forefinger as Fig. 1. Lower the thumb of the left hand on to the forefinger and roll the silk *and* the fur in a clockwise direction, as per Fig. 2. This is the action which wraps the fur round the silk, and it should be repeated with additional fur until a sufficient length of the silk has been covered. Press the finger and thumb together firmly during the rolling, opening them at the end of each individual roll. I stress this point so that you will not keep the finger and thumb together and just roll the fur backwards and forwards. It will be obvious that if rolling in one direction wraps the fur round the silk, rolling it back again will tend to unwrap it!

The dubbing should now look like Fig. 3, and is then wound towards the eye of the hook, not forgetting to leave enough space at the eye end for any wings and hackles that have to be tied in. The spacing of the winds will regulate the thickness of the body, and one usually overlaps them at the shoulder of the fly so that extra thickness is given at this point, Fig. 4. It is customary to give a tinsel rib of some sort to a dubbing body, and this is, of course, tied in at the tail before starting on the dubbing. This completes the durability of the body, and by the method I have shown it is possible to make bodies light and translucent, or thick and shaggy, that will put up with an almost unlimited amount of use. If the latter type of body is required, say, for a salmon fly, it is still far better to apply only a little dubbing to the silk at a time, adding more until a good thick "barrel" is achieved. After this is wound round the hook-shank, fibres can be pulled out from it with one's dubbing needle to give the hackle effect often needed.

If one is using a fur which has to be cut from the skin before use, it should be cut so that the staple is as long as possible. If the fibres are cut off so that they are only about $\frac{1}{8}$ in. long, the difficulty of wrapping them around the silk is greatly increased.

It is also a fact that some furs are more easily applied than others. Seal's fur, for instance, being more difficult than rabbit or hare, etc. This is due to the fibres of the seal's fur being stiffer and more springy than the others. The procedure is exactly the same for all, however, and it just means that the points I have emphasised must be more strictly observed with the difficult furs.

Among the many very good suggestions given to me by Capt. the Hon. R. Coke is his method of putting on dubbing bodies.

This method is particularly useful for those short-fibred dubbings which do not lend themselves easily to the "spinning" or rolling method I described. The procedure is as follows:

The fly is formed to the stage where the dubbing is required,

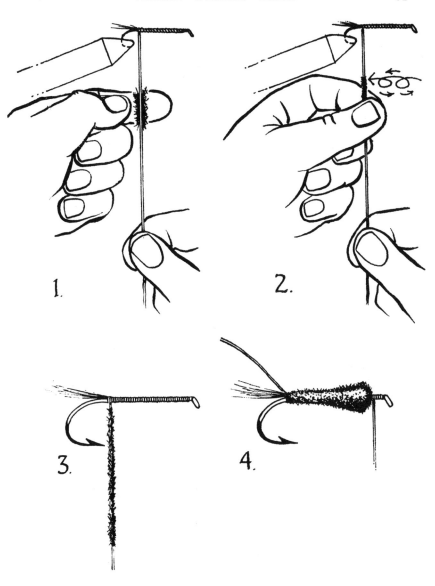

1.

2.

3.

4.

which would bring the tying silk to the tail usually. At this point another piece of well-waxed tying silk is tied in. Place a portion of the dubbing between the two silks, and then twist them together embracing the dubbing. The silks and dubbing are then wound to form the body, care being taken to see that the silks remain twisted together. Finish off with the original tying silk and cut off the end of the subsidiary piece.

This brings me to a tip passed on to me by N. F. Bostock, an associate of the late G. E. M. Skues. Any material which has a twist imparted to it, as this method calls for, should be wound in the opposite direction to the twist imparted. In other words, if the two silks are twisted together anti-clockwise to embrace the dubbing, they will not untwist when wound clockwise to form the body. This obviates the necessity of retwisting the silks during the process of forming the body. It will also be found useful when bodies are being formed of floss silks which have a twist in them when taken from the reel. Winding them on in one direction will continue to twist the silk into a tight cord, whereas winding them on in the opposite direction will untwist it so that a flat, well-shaped body is achieved. A small point, but a time saver.

CHAPTER 12. *MIXING DUBBINGS (FURS) FOR BODIES & STORING FOR EASY ACCESS*

It is often necessary, to achieve some particular shade, that two or more furs have to be mixed together. This mostly happens when some particular shade of olive is required, and if one has two or three packets of dyed olive, ranging from light to dark, many variations can be produced.

These can also be tinted further with browns, reds, orange, etc., if warmer shades are required, and a very good fiery brown can be produced by mixing chocolate, red and orange.

It will, of course, be apparent that there is no end to the colours one can achieve.

The secret of success is to do only a little at a time. It is also important that the correct ratio of ingredients should be adhered to. A small portion of the smallest ingredient, about the size of a pea, should be selected, and teased out to make as large a bulk as possible, so that it is more like a piece of fluff. The correct proportion of the next ingredient should be treated in the same manner. The two heaps of dubbing, when sufficiently opened out, should then be placed one on top of the other, and thoroughly mixed together by breaking and refolding until a more or less uniform colour is obtained.

When the pile is well mixed, small sections should be broken off and treated as was the pea-sized portion at the beginning. These should be mixed individually until the whole pile has been treated, and then all the separate piles of "fluff" mixed together again.

By this means it is possible to obtain one uniform colour, provided that clashing colours are not used, of course. I doubt very much if a very good grey could be obtained by trying to mix a

83

black and a white. It is, however, possible to blend suitable colours so that a uniform shade is obtained.

When it is necessary to blend fluorescent material into a dubbing, it is better to use the wool rather than a floss. The wool should be cut in strips of about ¾ in., and then teased out into a very fine fluff. In this form it is very easy to mix into the main dubbing.

It often happens that, when one comes to the actual mixing, it is found that the staple of one ingredient is longer than the other. While it will not altogether prevent the mixing of the two ingredients, it is much easier to mix them if the fibres of each are more or less the same length. Therefore, the dubbing with the longer fibres should be cut across several times with a pair of sharp scissors until it is reduced to about the same consistency of the other fur to be mixed.

Loose dubbing left on the fly tying bench can easily be blown away or get mixed up with other materials unless stored properly, although this storing should not be such that the furs are not readily available.

The best method and the most usual is a flat wooden or strong cardboard box with circular holes cut in the top about ½″ to ¾″ in diameter. The holes should be in rows with about ½″ between each. All one has to do then is push a different colour of fur into each hole, putting in sufficient fur so that it just "humps" above the level of the hole. As one picks off the small quantities used each time, the natural springiness of the fur will keep the "hump" just above the surface. The fur should be picked up with tweezers each time, to ensure that not too much is taken.

If one wishes to leave the fur in the packets in which they are purchased, usually cellophane envelopes, they should be left sealed and just a small triangle cut off one corner. The aforementioned springiness of the fur will push a small portion through the gap made, and the fur can be used without distributing most of it around the bench.

The most prevalent cause of distortion in tinsel bodies is the method by which the tinsel is first tied in. Unless it is so fixed that it can be wound evenly from the very start, an unsightly lump is formed at the tail end, and the spirals will not lie absolutely flat on the silk bed. The ribbing tinsel must also be tied in so that it starts neatly and has a good appearance at the tail end.

I have my own methods of achieving these objects, and although they may not be quite orthodox, if they are successful I am sure this will be overlooked. I feel rather strongly on this subject, as a clumsy tinsel body will ruin the appearance of any fly, no matter how well the rest of it may be made.

We have made the illustrations as large as we can for reasons of clarity, omitting items which do not concern the subject. We have included the tail so that the reader can know which aspect he is viewing.

Start the fly in the usual way, forming the tag (if it is a salmon fly), and tying in the tail. The latter should be so fixed that the turns of silk holding it are right up against the tag, with no gap. The ribbing is then tied in *underneath* the body, and pushed away to the left. The tinsel for the body is now cut off, and the usual diagonal cut made across it as shown in Figs. 1 & 2.

This is now placed underneath the body as Fig. 1 (seen from above), and one turn of silk taken round it and the hook shank to hold it in position. Fig. 2. The cut edge of the tinsel should be at right angles to the hook shank, *and this is most important*, so that the remaining length of tinsel will be angled to the right of the tyer. The importance of this will be seen as soon as one starts to wind the tinsel.

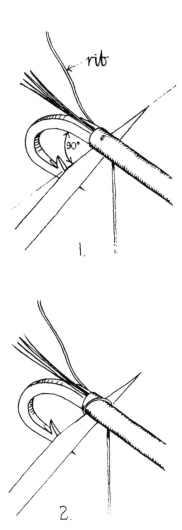

The cut end is then curled up and over the body, and two very tight turns made with the tying silk to hold it in position. Fig. 3. A piece of floss silk is now tied in at the shoulder of the fly, wound down to the tinsel and back again so that a smooth body of the desired thickness is achieved. Also as Fig. 3.

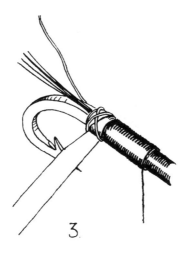

3.

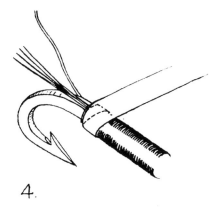

4.

One complete turn of the tinsel is now taken round the body, covering the point of the cut end of tinsel. Looking down, the tinsel should now be as Fig. 4. It will be observed that the diagonal is still apparent, and this is very important as the next turn of the tinsel must be taken to follow this line, and it will also give the angle at which the tinsel must be held for the subsequent turns. Therefore, turn number two will be as Fig. 5. Each turn of tinsel must lie *edge to edge* with the preceding one. Any overlapping will distort the tinsel, and any gap will be unsightly. The tinsel must be pulled very tightly during the winding, and that is why it is so very important that the pointed end be tied in very securely at the start.

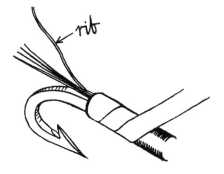

5.

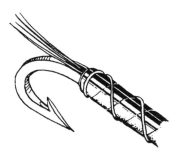

6

When the shoulder is reached, two turns of silk are put round the tinsel, and the surplus *broken* off. Breaking it off forms a ragged edge which will not slip out easily. If you prefer to cut it off, do not do so close up to the tying silk. The small surplus then remaining can be doubled back and fixed with a turn of silk.

Now back to the rib. This, you will remember, was tied in underneath the body. It is now wound one complete turn round the extreme edge of the tinsel body, and this should cover any gap between the tag and body. Bring it right round to the front, and then start the spiral as shown in Fig. 6. It is essential that the turns of this spiral shall all slope evenly and at the same angle. If they do not, this means that the tension of the rib is not equal along its entire length, and eventually the rib will slacken and lose its uniformity. When the end of the body is reached, the rib should be tied in underneath, and the surplus cut off.

It will be observed that in neither the script nor the illustrations has any butt been introduced. This is to point out that it is possible to form these tinsel bodies without the necessity of any butt being put in to conceal any untidiness at this point. This is an important factor when tying low-water patterns, for instance, although if a butt is used the procedure is not altered in any way.

If one uses wool for a tag, or ties a salmon fly with one or more items in the tail, an unsightly bump can form at the tail end of the tinsel body.

This bump cannot be avoided unless the tag and body are one smooth unit, so on small flies it is best to run the tag material the entire length of the body. It must be bound tightly and smoothly on top of the hook-shank with close turns of silk so that the tinsel will lie evenly. When the tag material will not reach the entire length of the body, and on larger flies, a short length of thin floss should be tied in at the shoulder and wound over the hook-shank and surplus tag material so that a smooth, even shape is formed, on which the tinsel can be wound easily and without distortion.

The following method of making tinsel bodies may appeal to some readers. It was among the many sent to me by Capt. the Hon. R. Coke.

The idea here is to use narrow or fairly narrow tinsel on all but very large salmon flies. This is tied in at the shoulder instead of the tail, and then wound to the tail and back again, winding very tightly and evenly with no overlap. It is essential that the jaws of one's vice grip the hook tightly, as there can be considerable leverage during this winding. It may be desirable to pad the hook-shank very lightly, and this should be done with split floss silk of white or grey, also wound very tightly and evenly.

I have found this to be a most excellent method for making tinsel bodies on small flies, as it produces a perfectly smooth body, completely devoid of bumps or distortion of any kind.

After winding the ribbing tinsel, if any, Capt. Coke advocates the use of a transparent cellulose paint to prevent tarnish.

Tinsel can be polished before winding by pulling it through a folded rag on which some wetted plate powder has been smeared. It is then finished off by drawing it through a piece of folded chamois-leather, without powder, of course. A final polish with the chamois can be given after the body is wound.

The above method produces a bright, smooth tinsel body, with no gaps or lumps, and should be no thicker in appearance than those made in the orthodox manner. I would like to add that a very neat appearance at the tail end is assured.

CHAPTER 14. *MAKING TANDEM HOOK MOUNTS FOR LURES, ETC.*

Many fly tyers experience difficulty in making a multi-hook lure which can be relied upon.

These multi-hook lures are mostly used for sea-trout fishing, but smaller types can be used in lakes and reservoirs, while larger editions are often used for salmon fishing. They consist of two or three hooks in tandem, whipped to gut or nylon, with a long over-wing, Fig. 1. They are sometimes called "Demons" or "Terrors", and have their counterpart in the American streamer type of fly. They differ in the respect that the latter are usually tied on a single long-shanked hook.

Orthodox dressings are mostly used, two of the most popular being the "Peter Ross" and "Alexandra", although there is no limit to the variations which may be applied. An "Alexandra" would have its two or three hooks dressed with the usual flat silver body, and the long fibres of green peacock herl dressed over an under-wing of red goose or swan. Jungle cock eyes and a crest over the top are optional.

So much for the type of fly. The difficulty which arises is how to whip the hooks on to the gut so that they will stay put. The rear hooks are usually of the eyeless variety, but this is not essential as the gut can be threaded through the loop of an eyed hook, so that it lies flat on the shank. It is best to start with the rear hook first.

If the hooks are whipped on tightly and evenly there should be no trouble, but any slackness or uneven whipping can result in a lost fish.

Place the rear hook in the vice and wind the tying silk evenly from the bend to the end of the shank. The length of gut is then

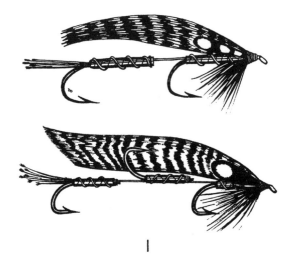

placed on top of the hook, and the tying silk wound in very tight, close turns back to the bend of the hook, and then back to the front end of the hook-shank again. Each turn must be very tight and close up against its neighbour. Uneven turns can result in the silk going slack. It is this tightness and uniformity which ensure that the hook will not slip. A couple of half-hitches are now made round the hook and the gut and the silk cut off.

If it is a three-hook lure being made, the middle hook is placed in the vice and a silk bed wound on as before. The gut is then placed on top with the rear hook to the top, and this will result in the centre hook being on top when the lure is completed, Fig. 1. The gut is now whipped to the centre hook as before. Now make the two half-hitches and cut off the tying silk. These half-hitches are necessary, as it is very difficult to make a whip finish with the end of the gut sticking out.

The front (eyed) hook is now put in the vice, and the procedure carried out as before. When all the hooks are tied on, their bindings must be well soaked in clear Cellire varnish, which must be allowed to dry hard before the bodies of the fly are put on.

If gut is used, this may be softened slightly in water before it is tied on, but if it is nylon, the portions which will be tied on to the hook-shank may be bitten lightly to form serrations on which the silk will grip. Twisted gut or nylon can be used to good effect, not only for extra strength, as the indentations formed by the twisting give the silk something to grip on.

Although this method may not seem to give a very robust anchorage for the hooks, it is surprising how tenacious close-whipped silk can be. Take half a dozen tight turns of silk round two closed fingers, and it will be found impossible to part them or break the silk.

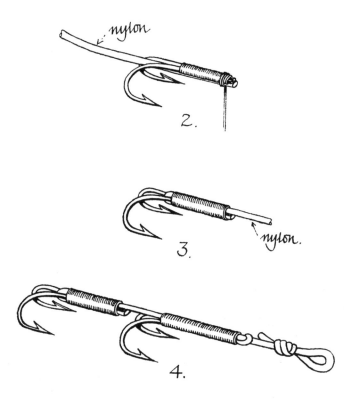

Sometimes these lures are made with double hooks, particularly for salmon lures, only two doubles being used. With these it is possible to make an almost slip-proof lure. The method is as follows:

The rear double is placed in the vice and the tying silk wound up and down the hook-shank as before. One end of the length of nylon is then pushed through the bends of the hook until its end reaches the end of the hook-shank (Fig. 2). This is then fixed with a couple of turns of the tying silk. The long end is then doubled over and brought down on to the hook-shank as Fig. 3, both sections of the nylon then being firmly tied in with the tying silk, which is wound down to the bend and back again. Take a half-hitch or two round nylon and hook at this point and cut off the tying silk.

The front hook is then placed in the vice and the free end of the nylon passed through its eye so that it protrudes sufficiently for a loop to be tied in it. It is then whipped to the hook as before. Incidentally, it is most important that these double hooks have the silk bed wound on first, so that the nylon is not whipped to the bare hook. The whippings are varnished as before, and a loop can be formed in the free end of the nylon. It will then be observed that even if the front hook should slip during use, it will be stopped by the rear hook, which is held firmly in the doubled end of the nylon. The completed mount is as Fig. 4. I think the illustration shows this quite clearly, and even if the front loop should be broken at any time, the cast can still be tied on to the eye of the front hook as normally.

The smaller lures can be tied by this method, using a small double at the rear and a single or singles in front of it.

Another most excellent method of making tandem hooks was given to me by Mr. A. K. Iles, of Fairford. The two hooks are whipped to fine trace wire, or stout nylon can be used, and the procedure is as follows:

Cut the wire (or nylon) so that it is a little more than double the length you require the tandem hooks to be. Divide the wire exactly in half by folding, and whip one half on top of the rear hook, as shown, (Fig. 5) the half being tied down, being pushed through the eye of the hook first. The wire is then bound tightly to the hook, as I have described earlier in this chapter and then varnished.

Now push the rear end of the wire through the eye of hook and bind this down and varnish it. We now have one hook with the two ends of wire protruding from the eye, both firmly bound down on to it. It is the binding down separately that gives the two ends of wire their immovable fixture, as stage two (Fig. 6).

The front hook is now put into the vice ready for the protruding ends of wire to be bound to it. Whether the rear hook points up or down is left to the preference of the tyer, but for the purposes of this illustration the rear hook is shown in the "up" position.

The two ends of wire are now bound down on top of the front hook, but in this instance the ends are *not* pushed through the eye of the hook (Fig. 7).

Well varnish the silk bindings once again and then cut off the surplus wire so that the two ends project about $\frac{1}{4}$ in. beyond the eye. These two ends are then doubled back over the hook and firmly bound down as per Fig. 8.

To make the fixture even more breakproof, each arm of the wire can be tied down separately, including the bent back end.

All the silk bindings should now be well varnished once again, building up several coats of the varnish, which should be allowed several days to harden. It is then ready for tails, bodies and hackles, and in use will be found practically indestructible.

The short lengths of wire between the two hooks can be twisted together before attaching the front hook, but this is not necessary with the nylon.

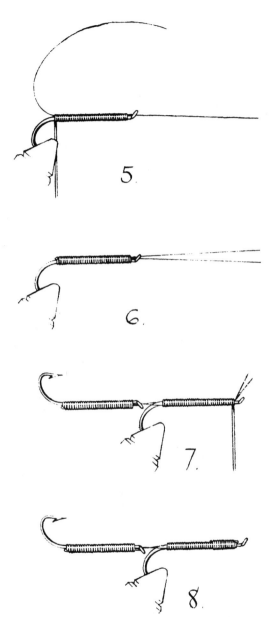

5.

6.

7.

8.

CHAPTER 15. MAKING HAIR BODIES & HEAD OF "MUDDLER MINNOW"

This type of body is not in regular use in the United Kingdom, but in North America it is a favourite medium for the large lures used to attract large- and small-mouthed bass.

The reason for this is its floating qualities and the fact that it can be trimmed into shape after application. By this means, lures representing frogs, mice, shrews, etc., can be realistically reproduced, which can be worked across the surface of the water in a most lifelike manner.

The material used is the *body* hair of the common red deer, and as this varies from deep red brown through grey to a pale buff, several colour variations are possible. For instance, buff, brown, buff and so on will give a barred effect if required.

The reason I stress that it is the body hair which must be used is because it is the texture of these hairs which give the material its floating ability. The individual fibres are very stiff and quite thick. It is these qualities which enable the lure to float, and make possible the particular method of application. The finer hairs, say from the tail, will not spin round the hook-shank as will the stiffer and thicker body hairs.

The actual method of application is very simple and requires very little practice. It is as follows:

Place the hook in the vice (usually a stout long-shanked one), and fix the tying silk at the *bend* of the hook. No silk is run down the shank (Fig. 1).

Cut a small bunch of body fibres from the skin and hold them over the hook immediately above where the silk is tied in, and in line with the shank (Fig. 2).

Now take *two* loose turns round the fur and the hook-shank,

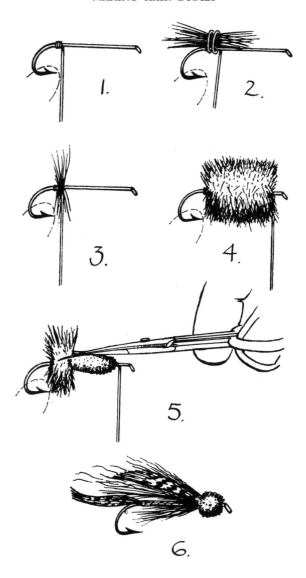

1.

2.

3.

4.

5.

6.

just firm enough to hold the fur on to the hook, so that the fingers holding the fur can be released. When the fingers are released pull the silk tight and the fur will flare round the hook-shank just like a hackle (Fig. 3).

The silk should now be behind this "hackle", so, still keeping it tight, pass it through the "hackle", make a half-hitch round the hook-shank and press this close up to the "hackle".

The procedure is now repeated with another bunch of hairs, and another half-hitch as before. Carry on until the necessary amount of hook-shank has been covered, and the result should be a "flue-brush" anything from 1 in. to 1½ in. in diameter (4).

This "brush" can be trimmed to shape, using a sharp pair of pointed scissors, resulting in a bristle body of most lifelike appearance (Fig. 5).

It is, of course, possible to dye the lighter-coloured hairs, and if a really dark body is required, the darker hairs can be dyed various browns, greens, or black.

A stout tying silk should be used so that the turns of silk can be pulled really tight, and although I advocate that the hook-shank should be left bare before commencing, an open layer of silk can be put over it when one has become adept at flaring the hairs. It is much easier to do on the bare hook.

This is the method used for making the distinctive head of the "Muddler Minnow". In this instance, however, only the front of the fly is treated as described, and this is trimmed giving the effect shown in Fig. 6.

CHAPTER 16. MAKING DETACHED BODIES

In spite of the fact that the making of detached body flies creates a certain amount of difficulty, they are still popular, and I get many requests for the best ways of making them up. The advent of the long-shanked light wire hook has done much to oust this type of fly, but there is no doubt that the detached body looks very realistic.

Cork is a very popular material for making these bodies, especially for mayflies, and there are two methods of applying it. One is to use a fairly thin sheet of cork folded in half, or two pieces of greater thickness placed side by side. The method of fixing them to the hook is the same for both, and is as follows:

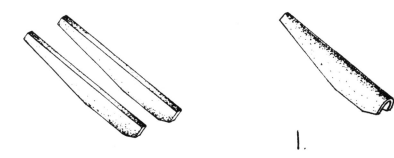

1.

If the two separate pieces are used, they are first cut to the approximate shape of the fly body as shown in Fig. 1. The shape of cork required to be folded is also shown. They are then trimmed to the exact shape. The tying silk is then tied in near the bend of the hook and wound to a point near the eye of the hook, or to a point where it is desired to tie in the body (Fig. 2). The colour of this tying silk should be neutral, and as near to the colour of the cork as possible. The two pieces of cork are now smeared on their inside surfaces with Cellire cement, and two or three turns of silk taken round their front end, placing them on the hook-shank so that they overlap it slightly, as shown in Fig. 2. Continue winding the silk at fairly wide intervals so that a criss-cross effect may be achieved instead of a close one, until point "A" is reached. Now separate the two sections with a dubbing needle and insert the tail fibres (Fig. 3). Position these and then squeeze the two sides together. Now continue to wind the tying silk to the tail end of the body, and then back again to the front, keeping the same interval of width (Fig. 4). Allow the cement to set, and then finish the fly by adding wings and hackles.

To make detached bodies for small flies, the best material to use is nylon monofilament of a thickness or slightly thicker than the hook-shank. This is tied tightly to the top of the hook-shank, and any excess of length clipped off. Apply a drop of cement to the tip of the nylon and fasten on the tail fibres, after which a piece of floss silk is tied in at the same point. Hold the nylon in the left hand and then wind the body material to the shoulder of the fly, incorporating the hook-shank in the windings at the appropriate place. Ribbing of silk or tinsel can also be added to these bodies if required. The finger and thumb holding the nylon can be brought into play to assist the winding of the body silks or ribbing.

I have also received several suggestions as to materials which can be used for detached bodies, one being surgical oiled silk which is obtainable from chemists' suppliers. This material is cut into strips as wide as the body required, and then rolled round a needle to give it the required shape. The tail fibres are placed in

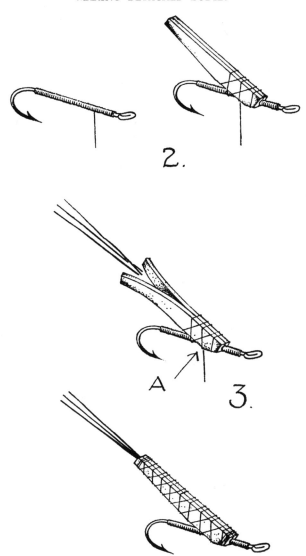

2.

A 3.

4.

the narrow end of the cylinder, and fixed with knotted tying silk, one end of which is continued round and down the body to form the rib. The thicker end is then tied tightly to the hook-shank. This material makes a very light, airtight body which is not only most translucent, but very natural looking.

Another ingenious suggestion was the use of feather quills. I have found that the best ones come from the quill tips of such flank feathers as brown mallard or teal, as these are both well shaped and translucent. Fig. 5 shows the portion to be used, and this is tied in with its closed end forming the tail end of the body. Tails and ribbings can be added as for the other detached bodies described in the foregoing.

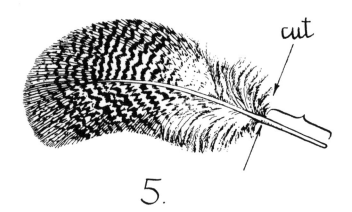

cut

5.

Another most original method of making a detached-bodied fly was sent to me by W. R. Coffey, of Montreal. The originator of the method was Harry Darbee, a very well-known American fisherman and fly tyer.

Darbee's unique method requires only a single feather for body, wings and tail, and the feather is prepared as follows, and as shown in the first two illustrations.

All surplus fluff and fibres are removed, and the remaining fibres stroked outwards and then downwards, the feather ending

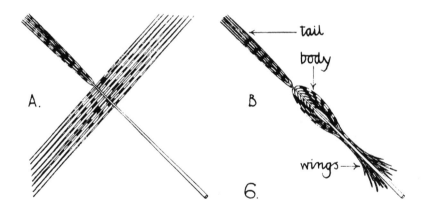

up as Fig. 6B. The section of quill between the "wings" is then tied on to the hook as per Fig. 7A, and when the surplus quill is cut off a side view of our fly should be as Fig. 7B.

We now have a fly with cocked wings, but there is no reason why they may not be set in the open or "spent" positions.

Fibres can be cut from the tail section if it is too bushy.

A hackle is added in the usual way (Fig. 8A), two turns at the rear of the wings and two in front, and a finished fly should look like Fig. 8B.

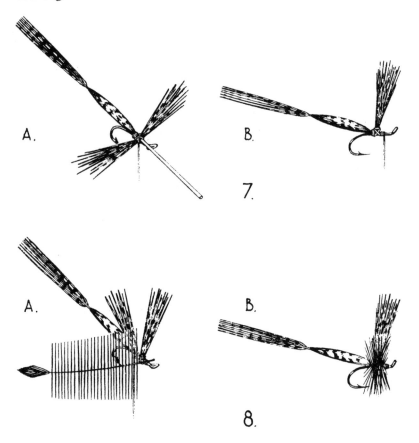

The beauty of this fly is its extreme lightness, not only because only one feather is used for wings, body and tail, but because it can be tied on to the smallest dry-fly hooks.

Darbee designed this fly for fish rising on a polished surface, and although it is elongated like a natural, because it weighs only about one quarter as much as a traditional fly, it floats down on to the water like gossamer.

I find that this method will produce a fine extra-light mayfly.

I use a No. 13 up-eyed hook, and feathers from the breast of teal, wood-duck, and mallard are ideal, both dyed and undyed. For hackles I use badger, grizzle, and various dyed shades in the olive group, and these can be of a size normally used for small dry-flies.

It is the use of these small hackles which gives the fly its very natural appearance, and their extreme lightness makes them ideal for those streams which have long slow glides where a minimum of disturbance is essential.

Since *Fly Tying Problems* was first published, science has come to the aid of the fly tyer once again, in the shape (literally) of moulded plastic bodies that are both realistic, light and translucent. They are also hollow, and providing the tyer ensures that they are airtight when tied on, they will float indefinitely.

Their size makes them ideal for use as detached bodies for mayflies and sedges, and they are particularly effective for "spent" patterns.

The usual long-shank mayfly hook may, of course, be dispensed with, Nos. 12 or 13 Redditch size being quite large enough.

Tails, if required, are added by cutting a very small hole at the extreme tip of the body, and then threading the tails point first through the main opening (Fig. 10). The hole in the tip must then be sealed with cement or clear varnish, otherwise the body will not be airtight.

The body, including the butts of the tail fibres, is then bound down on top of the hook in the middle of the shank. As fairly long fibres are used for tails on mayflies, there is always plenty of surplus at the butt end to be tied in.

Tying the body in the middle of the hook-shank leaves plenty of room for wings (if any are required), and hackle, and the turns of the latter can be kept to a minimum. This is because the hackle is not required to keep the fly afloat, so therefore its fibres can fulfil the true function—representation of the legs.

Lifelike segments are moulded into the bodies during manufacture, so no ribbing is required. The meticulous tyer can, if he wishes, accentuate the rib markings with varnish, and the result is really most lifelike.

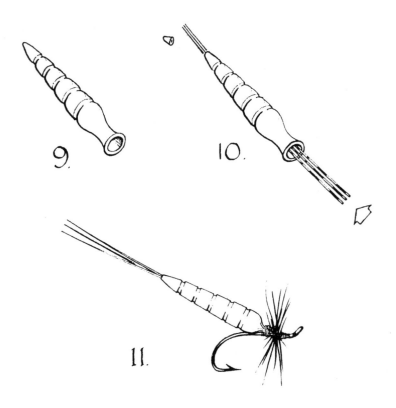

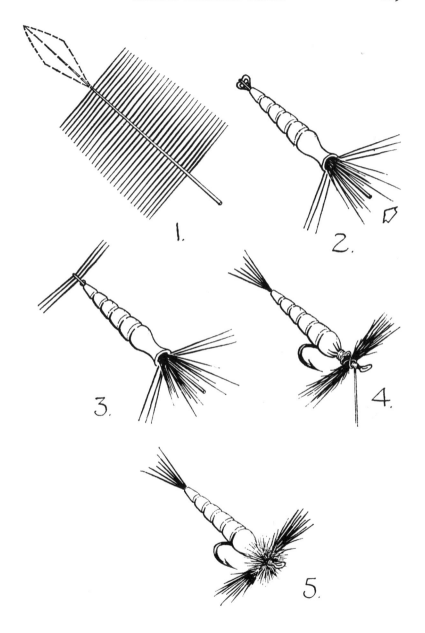

1.

2.

3.

4.

5.

Whilst discussing this chapter with Donald Downs, he came up with his own idea of how these moulded plastic bodies could be utilised. A very simple method too.

First he took a large hackle (other feathers could also be used for this purpose), drew down the fibres and then cut off the tip (Fig. 1). The hackle was then inserted tip first, until sufficient fibres came through to form the tail (Figs. 2 and 3). Drawing the feather or hackle back again slightly puts these fibres into the tail position as shown in Fig. 4. The body is then tied down on top of the hook shank, the hackle stalk cut off, and the protruding fibres tied in the "spent" position as per Fig. 4. They could also be tied in the upright position if so desired. All one has to do then is add a hackle, and the finished fly is as Fig. 5.

CHAPTER 17. HOOKS—TERMINOLOGY

I have many requests for information on hooks—the best to use for different types of fishing. Salmon flies do not present much difficulty as far as hooks are concerned, as the range is very limited these days, but trout flies can be tied on a wide variety of irons.

The kind of fish to be caught, where it lives, and the type of fly to be used, must, of course, determine the type of hook to use. A heavy hook in clear, placid water is as much out of place as a fine wire hook would be in heavy water where large fish can be expected. Furthermore, different kinds of hooks must be used for different flies, streamer patterns, nymphs, etc., as no hook is appropriate for all fly-fishing conditions.

The range of all types of hooks is much smaller than before the war, when it was possible to get a greater variety. If anyone worked out a new design which the manufacturers thought practical, they were often prepared to manufacture and market it. Such is not the case these days, as present-day costs of retooling, etc., make the introduction of a new pattern a costly business, and not a practical proposition unless a very big quantity is made. However, the range of types available for fly tying is still quite extensive, and one soon decides on preferred patterns for one's types of fishing. Fig. 1 illustrates the descriptive points of modern usage, and in this case it is a forged upturned-eye pattern.

Salmon flies can be divided up into four main groups: those using standard hooks which have a Dublin or Limerick Bend; summer or low-water hooks which are of lighter wire and longer in the shank for the same gape; dry-fly hooks which are of very light wire and which can also be used for low-water flies, and

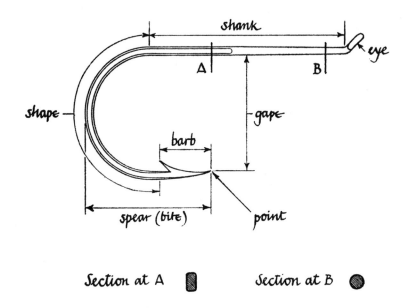

Section at A   Section at B

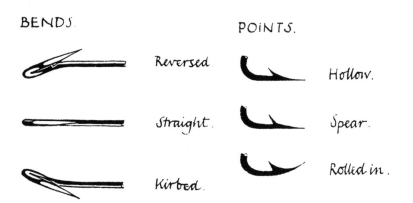

SHAPES

EYES.

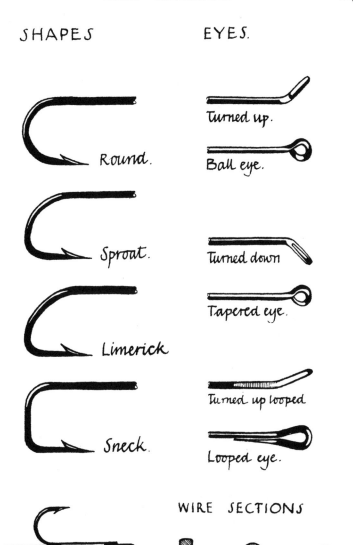

Round.

Turned up.

Ball eye.

Sproat.

Turned down

Tapered eye.

Limerick

Sneck.

Turned up looped

Looped eye.

WIRE SECTIONS

Forged.   Regular.   Oval.

trebles for use with the now very popular tube flies. The standard and low-water hooks are also used as doubles.

The "shape" is the index to the hook pattern and I have illustrated one or two of the most popular of these. Incidentally, the "shape" is quite often referred to as the "bend". "Bend" really refers to any lateral offset to the point and barb, i.e. when the point is offset to the right it is called a "reverse bend" and when it is offset to the left it is called a "kirbed bend". Another misnomer is that of "snecked bend" instead of "kirbed", although it has been used so much now that it is an accepted description. The purpose of these bends is to direct the penetration of the point at an angle to the shank, which helps to prevent the release of the hook as the point and the shank are not parallel.

For dry-fly fishing, one of the best patterns to use is one with a sproat shape and turned-up eye, a slight reverse bend, and, of course, made of light wire. An alternative, and second in popularity, is the same type of hook with a turned-down eye, although I think that much of its popularity is due to the fact that it is considered easier by some tyers to dress a fly on a downturned eye hook. Hooks with the round shape are also popular for dry-flies in its smaller sizes, but as the wire increases in weight in the larger sizes they are also admirable for wet-flies.

A good hook for all-round types of wet-flies is the Limerick pattern, which is usually of quite stout wire. Another type of hook, which is self-descriptive, is the long-shanked. They are obtainable with either up- or down-eyes.

I am grateful to Mr. S. A. Shrimpton, managing director of Messrs. Allcock & Co. Ltd., for the following notes on hook nomenclature.

"BEND". This is definitely a trade term for the shape of the hook, such as kirby bend, Limerick-bend, round bend, sneck bend, etc. To shape the hook, barbed and pointed wires were pulled round on a hand "peg-bend"; later the bend was fixed in a hand-operated machine, and the wire pulled round to shape.

As regards the different parts of a hook, we usually describe as the "depth" that part which you call "spear". The machine point (as distinct from the old hand-filed point) is generally termed "spear point" so that there could be no confusion.

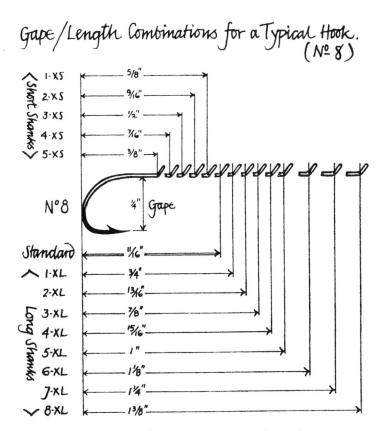

Gape/Length Combinations for a Typical Hook.
(N° 8)

1·XS	5/8"
2·XS	9/16"
3·XS	1/2"
4·XS	7/16"
5·XS	3/8"

Short Shanks

N° 8   1/4" Gape

Standard	11/16"
1·XL	3/4"
2·XL	13/16"
3·XL	7/8"
4·XL	15/16"
5·XL	1"
6·XL	1 1/8"
7·XL	1 1/4"
8·XL	1 3/8"

Long Shanks

NOTE. Measurements do not include the hook eye.

Further variations (not shown) include differences in the gauge of wire, to suit hook purposes, ie., for dry, wet & salmon flies.

Many dressings given in books do not state which tying silk should be used.

Tinsel-bodied flies, of course, do not present much difficulty, as the only place where the silk might show is at the head or through the hackle. Therefore, the colour to choose would be the colour of the hackle. Black for "Butcher", for instance, and red for "Bloody Butcher", "Red Spinner" or "Wickham's Fancy", and so on.

With dubbing bodies, I always use a colour approaching that of the dubbing fur used, claret for "Mallard and Claret", yellow for "Invecta", and olive for "Rough Olive", etc.

If a body is formed which will become semi-transparent when wet, a colour should be used which will have a neutral effect, such as white or grey.

Waxing tying silk is the initial operation of all fly tying, and although a simple operation, it is a necessary one, and there is no doubt that well waxed silk goes a long way to ensure success during subsequent stages of procedure.

Professional fly tyers wax their silk to the degree that even if they let go of it altogether, the adhesiv equalities of the amount of wax they have applied will keep it in position and hold any materials that have been applied.

To do this a small head of wax is kept permanently in the palm of the hand to keep it soft, and the tying silk is drawn vigorously through this so that a heavy coating is applied. This cuts out time spent on half hitches or using weights to hold the silk and materials in place. As this consideration is not as necessary to the amateur tyer, the silk need not be treated so drastically for his needs, but it is still essential that the silk be given a good covering coat of wax.

The simplest way to do this is as follows: Draw about 12 in. of silk from the reel (through the bobbin holder if one is being used), and hold it in place on the piece of wax by the thumb of the other hand. Now pull it *very rapidly* across the wax three or four times. The speed of the pull creates friction between the silk and the wax, the heat melting the latter so that it coats round the silk. The more times one does this, the thicker will be the wax coating. To pull the silk slowly is useless, for not only does the wax not melt, the silk is prone to stick in the wax and break, or it will be weakened and break during the tying.

One of my mentors during the early days of my fly tying, told me that if silk was properly waxed, it was not necessary to varnish the head of the fly, particularly small dry flies. I have found this to be true, but it is not an assumption I would like to lay down as a hard and fast rule. It does however, accentuate how useful and important the waxing is, and although there is a school of thought which advocates the dispensing of waxing altogether, it is not one with which I agree. Even if it is only for the fact that waxed silk is less likely to rot than if it is used unwaxed.

BI-VISIBLE FLIES. These are designed to improve the visibility of flies to both angler and fish, particularly when using dark flies in poor light. It merely entails the adding of a white or light-coloured hackle to the front of the hackle called for in the dressing. In other words, if a white hackle was wound in front of the hackle used on the "Red Palmer" the fly would then be called a "Red Palmer Bi-visible".

BOBBIN HOLDER. A tool for holding a whole reel of silk during tying, dispensing the silk as required.

DETACHED BODY. The body of an artificial fly, complete in itself, tied on to the hook shank, but separate from it.

DRY FLY. A fly so dressed that it will remain afloat when in contact with the water.

DUBBING. See Fur Bodies.

DUBBING NEEDLE. Used to pick out fur fibres on a "dubbed" body, to simulate legs, feelers, etc.

FLUORESCENCE. Some fly-tying materials are now treated so as to have this property—the ability to reflect light rays during the hours of daylight—useful during dull days and heavy water conditions. It is not possible to get dark shades, such as black, only pastel shades of the primary colours, or variations of them, can be achieved. Manufactured fibres such as nylon react very well to this treatment, but natural materials such as hackles can be quite effective also.

FUR BODIES. These are formed by twisting or "dubbing" furs on to the tying silk, and then winding them round the hook-shank to form the body of the fly.

HACKLE. Feather wound round the hook-shank to represent the legs or wings of a fly.

HACKLE PLIERS. Used to grip the tip of the hackle to facilitate its winding.

HAIR BODIES. These are formed by using the stiffish body hairs of the common deer. They are spun on to form a "hackle" which is then cut to any desired body shape. This method is used not only because bulky bodies can be made up, but also for the extremely good floatability of this type of body.

HERLS. Short fibres or "flue" which stand out from individual feather fibres or quills. When these fibres or quills are wound round the hook-shank, the "flue" stands out at right-angles, imparting a certain amount of translucence to the solid body. Peacock and ostrich tail feather fibres are the two best examples of herls, but fibres from wing quills and tail feathers of many other birds are also used, heron, condor, goose and swan being very popular.

IRONS. This is the Old Scottish name for salmon-fly hooks and has now become general idiom for any type of hook.

LOW-WATER FLIES. Very lightly dressed salmon flies, the wing-tips of which are dressed well forward of the bend of the hook. They are used in summer or low-water conditions by means of the "greased line" method. So called because the whole of the line and the cast—to within 18 in. of the fly—is greased so that the fly does not sink very far below the surface.

MALLARD FEATHERS FOR WINGS. One often comes upon this term in the dressing of a fly, but as the mallard supplies so many for wings, some difficulty may be experienced in deciding which one to choose. The best thing I can do here is give the names of the best known flies which use different types of mallard feathers.

Bronze Mallard Shoulder Feathers. "Mallard and Claret" and all the other "Mallard" series of flies. "Connemara Black", "Golden Olive", "Fiery Brown", "Thunder and Lightning", "Blue

Charm", and nearly all other salmon flies which have mixed wings.

Grey Mallard Flank Feathers. This is a grey speckled feather similar to teal flank, but with much lighter markings. It is used for "John Spencer", "Queen of Waters", "Grizzly King", "Professor", and as a substitute for teal and pintail feathers in many salmon flies.

Grey Mallard Quill Feathers. These are the wing primary feathers, and can be used for nearly any fly which calls for a grey wing, particularly in the larger sizes, i.e. 'Silver Saltoun", "Wickham's Fancy", "Blae and Black", etc.

Blue/White Tipped Mallard Quill Feathers. These also come from the wing, the blue part of the quill being used for one of the best known of all flies—the "Butcher". Strips taken from the white tip of the feather are used for "Heckham and Red", and all the others of the "Heckham" series, "McGinty", "Jock", and, in fact, any fly which has a wing with a white tip. This includes small and low-water salmon flies where a white-tipped turkey tail feather would be too large.

MARRIED FIBRES. Fibres taken from different feathers and then joined together to form one whole wing section. Used mainly for mixed and built wing salmon flies.

PALMER FLY. Any fly which has the hackle wound from shoulder to tail. A fly so dressed is usually referred to as "tied Palmer".

PARACHUTE FLY. This term is used for flies with the hackle wound in a horizontal plane instead of round the hook-shank.

QUILL. Body: usually formed by one of the fibres from a peacock's tail, after the flue has been stripped from it. Strips cut from the centre quill of tail or wing quill feathers with a knife can also be used.

WINGS: when a dressing calls for a wing from a "quill", this means that the feather fibres from the quill are used for the wing.

RIBS. These can be formed of silk, herls or tinsels. On trout flies they are usually meant to simulate the segmentations of insect bodies, whereas on salmon flies their function is to strengthen the body material and protect any body hackle if used.

SILK BODIES. Strands of silk, usually floss, wound directly on to the hook-shank to form the body.

TAIL. See Whisks.

TAIL FEATHER. When a dressing calls for a wing or part of a wing from a tail feather, this means that the feather fibres from the tail are used. "Grouse and Green" uses feather fibres from the grouse tail.

TEAL FEATHERS FOR WINGS. As with the mallard, the teal supplies several feathers for wings. When a fly has a black-and-white barred feather for the wings, it is the breast or flank feather of the teal which is used. Such flies are "Peter Ross", "Teal and Green", "Teal and Blue" and all the others of the "Teal" series. The grey feathers of the wing can be used for such patterns as "Wickham's Fancy" or any other largish pattern requiring a grey wing.

TANDEM HOOKS. Two or more hooks whipped to gut, nylon monofilament, or wire, in line with each other. Used mostly for sea- and lake-trout lures, sometimes referred to as "Demons" and "Terrors". The now very popular "Worm Fly" is usually tied on a two-hook tandem.

TINSEL. Strips of flat metal and strands of silk covered with metal. Used for whole bodies or just for ribbing. When in doubt use a flat tinsel for a whole body, and the covered silk tinsel for ribbing.

TINSEL BODIES. Bodies made of metal strip wound the length of the hook-shank, used to impart "flash" to a fly, particularly those flies which are supposed to resemble a small fish.

TUBE FLIES. Flies which have the body hackle and wings (if any) tied on to a length of plastic or metal tubing. The hook is supplied by tying a double or treble hook to a length of gut, and passing it through the tube.

TYING SILK. Fine natural silk, by which all materials are tied to the hook.

WAX. This enables the tying silk to grip the materials firmly while the fly is being tied. Solid or liquid types can be used.

WET FLY. A fly so dressed that it will sink when cast.

WHIP FINISH. The best method of finishing off a fly. It consists of two or three turns of the tying silk laid over the end of the silk before it is pulled tight.

WHIP FINISHER. A tool so designed to simplify the application of the whip finish of the fly. It is only suitable for this purpose and cannot apply whip finishes to rods, hooks to gut or any other article which has a projection beyond the actual whip finish.

WHISKS. Fibres of feathers used to form the tail. If material such as wool or silk is used, they are more often referred to as a "tag" instead of a tail.

WINGS. Here is a list of the various types of wings used on trout and salmon flies.

Wet Fly. A flat wing sloping back over the body of the fly.

Double Split Wing Dry Fly. Formed of two sections each, taken from a pair of matched wing quills and tied in so that the tips point outwards.

Fan Wings. Formed of two small breast feathers, usually from the mallard drake, tied in to curve outwards.

Advanced Wing. Term used when the wing slopes over the eye of the fly instead of the body. Can be a flat wing or a double split wing.

Down Wing. Used for dry-flies which simulate the Sedge group, Stone flies and Alder flies.

Rolled Wing. These consist of a roll of feather fibres taken from a wing quill or tail. They are used for the down-wing types mentioned above, and for some well-known types of North Country upright-winged dry-flies.

Upright Wing. Any wing that stands upright from the body of the fly. They can be double split wings, fan wings, rolled wings, hackle point wings, etc.

Bunch Wings. Wings formed by a bunch of fibres cut from any feather. They can be tied upright, low over the body, advanced or split.

Split Wings. Any wings that have their points separated.

Hackle Point Wings. Almost self-explanatory. The tips of hackles are used to form the wings, two for most patterns, four for may-flies.

Spent Wings. Wings tied so that they lie flat on the water when the fly is cast—imitating the spent fly. Hackle points or hackle fibres are the most popular of this type.

Hackle Fibre Wings. Similar to "bunch wings" in so far that a bunch of hackle fibres is used for the wings.

Shaving Brush Wings. Hair or feather fibres tied in so that they point forward over the eye of the hook in line with the shank. Down-eyed hooks should be used to facilitate the tying on of the cast, or the tying silk should be so wound so as to form a slight split down the centre of the wing.

Hair Wings. Wings formed of animal fur fibres. Invariably down wings or wings of the "shaving brush" type.

Streamer Wings. Wings formed of whole hackles or long strips of other feathers, the tips of which project well beyond the bend of the hook.

Strip Wings. A term used for salmon-fly wings which are made of strips taken from one type of feather only.

Whole Feather Wings. Term used when a whole feather or two whole feathers back to back, form the wing of the fly.

Mixed Wings. Wings that are formed from the fibres of several different feathers, "married" together to form single whole sections.

Herl Wings. Wings that are formed with the feathers normally used for herl bodies. The "Alexandra" is the best-known example.

WING CASES. The "hump" incorporated in the dressings of

nymphs and beetle imitations to simulate the wing housing. They are usually formed of feather fibres tied in at one point, folded down on to the body and then tied in at another point. If fur or silk is used for the body, this should be thickened between these two points so as to accentuate the "hump".

VARNISH. This is applied to the final turns or whip finish of the fly, to prevent the silk unravelling during use. Clear varnish is usually used for dry-flies, while spirit and coloured varnishes are used for wet-flies and salmon flies.

It is as well to have some method of ensuring that bottles of varnish are not knocked over whilst actually tying. An accident of this nature could ruin many hours of work, or make valuable items of material unusable. A simple stand capable of taking a selection of varnishes and thinners, etc., was designed by Peter Deane and is illustrated below.

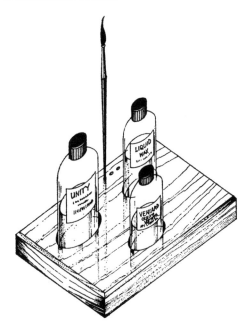

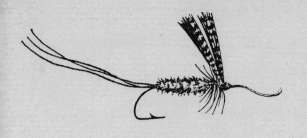

17th – 18th Century.

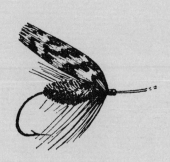
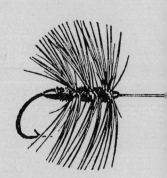

19th Century

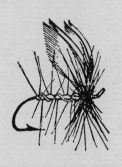

Early 20th Century